NOW WHAT?
CONFRONTING AND RESOLVING
ETHICAL QUESTIONS

For

Peter and Pamela Vose
Deborah Vose and Steven Roman
John Mackenzie and Susan Nybell
Rebecca Vose and Steven Schreckinger
Arthur and Margaret Vose

NOW WHAT?
CONFRONTING AND RESOLVING ETHICAL QUESTIONS

A HANDBOOK FOR TEACHERS

SARAH V. MACKENZIE
G. CALVIN MACKENZIE

CORWIN
A SAGE Company

For information:

Corwin
A SAGE Company
2455 Teller Road
Thousand Oaks, California 91320
(800) 233-9936
Fax: (800) 417-2466
www.corwin.com

SAGE India Pvt. Ltd.
B 1/I 1 Mohan Cooperative
Industrial Area
Mathura Road, New Delhi 110 044
India

SAGE Ltd.
1 Oliver's Yard
55 City Road
London EC1Y 1SP
United Kingdom

SAGE Asia-Pacific Pte. Ltd.
33 Pekin Street #02-01
Far East Square
Singapore 048763

Printed in the United States of America.

Library of Congress Cataloging-in-Publication Data

Mackenzie, Sarah V.
Now what? confronting and resolving ethical questions: A handbook for teachers/ Sarah V. Mackenzie, G. Calvin Mackenzie.
    p. cm.
Includes bibliographical references and index.
ISBN 978-1-4129-7084-6 (pbk.)
    1. Teachers—Professional ethics. 2. Teaching—Moral and ethical aspects. I. Mackenzie, G. Calvin. II. Title.

LB1779.M3295 2010
174'.937—dc22   2009035720

This book is printed on acid-free paper.

15   16   17   18   19   10   9   8   7   6   5   4   3   2

Acquisitions Editor:	Dan Alpert
Associate Editor:	Megan Bedell
Production Editor:	Eric Garner
Copy Editor:	Tomara Kafka
Typesetter:	C&M Digitals (P) Ltd.
Proofreader:	Sally Jaskold
Indexer:	Judy Hunt
Cover Designer:	Michael Dubowe

Contents

Preface

As teachers, and teachers of teachers, we spend the bulk of our time focusing on techniques of pedagogy and the substance of our subject matter. We try to teach *how* to teach and *what* to teach. But in the decades of our experience, we have come to learn that there is more to successful teaching than pedagogy and substantive expertise. Good teachers must also be practitioners of ethical propriety. Teacher self-esteem requires that. Effective schools require that. But, most importantly, students require that.

Teachers and school leaders cannot escape the need to cope with ethical challenges. They are simply an inevitable part of the professional lives we lead. No one who works in a school gets through a year without confronting difficult choices between right and wrong, dealing with a colleague or student who has acted irresponsibly, or feeling the temptation to bend the rules or the law for some perceived higher purpose.

But most teachers and school leaders have little formal preparation for these challenges and few reliable navigational aids when they confront them. It was this recognition that led us to write this book. We believe that it fills a significant vacuum in the preparation of teachers and administrators for the real lives they will lead in their schools. And it provides guidance for those already confronting rough seas.

This is not a treatise on ethics or an exercise in theorizing, though we have been blessed in preparing it by the excellent work of those theorists whose inquiries have raised the level of understanding and insight among all students of ethics, including us. Many of them are named in the citations throughout this book.

But our purpose here is more practical. We have drawn from our own experiences and from the much broader range of experiences among scores of teachers and school leaders who have shared with us the details of incidents in their own lives and their own schools. We suggest some important ethical principles at the outset of this book and we offer some guidelines for how one might think about a difficult ethical dilemma.

But we believe that the best way to heighten one's own ethical sensitivities is through practice. And we have provided dozens of cases, drawn from actual experience, to provide the grist for that kind of activity. What we hope to encourage is discussion. Put yourself in the place of the teachers and school leaders portrayed in these cases. What choices did they confront? What were the potential costs and benefits of each option for action? How would you have acted and why? We offer our own suggestions for some of these cases, though we wrap them in no pretense of perfection. For others, we leave readers to their own devices to assess and respond to the situations we pose.

We provide no "answers" to the questions these cases raise for the simple and important reason that we believe the best answers come from reflection and discussion, not from an answer key at the back of the book. Our fond hope—and our firm belief—is that by thinking and talking about these cases, many of which will strike chords of recognition among experienced teachers, readers will come away with a clearer sense of what constitutes an ethical issue and what sorts of responses are possible and prudent. We hope that we have provided a practical guide to practical learning.

While we take full responsibility for the contents of this book, we could not have done it alone and we did not. Nearly a hundred experienced educators provided invaluable assistance by telling us their own stories of difficult circumstances they faced and choices they had to make. These included graduate students in the Educational Leadership Program at the University of Maine, other teachers and school leaders from around the country, professional colleagues, and our brothers and sisters and their spouses in our large family where teaching is a common and treasured profession. We are deeply grateful to all of them for the time they spent with us in conversation about this project and for their candor, insights, and often, their self-criticism.

We are grateful as well for the support we have received from the universities where we teach, the University of Maine and Colby College, and from our colleagues and the administrations of them both. Directly and indirectly, our thinking about the issues addressed in this book has been shaped and refined by the wisdom we acquired in the daily conversations with those with whom we work. We happily and gratefully list here the names of those who helped us in preparing this book in the acknowledgments.

We wish as well to thank the good people at Corwin who shared our enthusiasm for this project from the start and who guided it smoothly from an idea to a book. Dan Alpert, our editor, served as midwife at the outset and wise counselor throughout. We also thank Megan Bedell, associate editor, who helped keep the project on track and Tomara Kafka who carefully and thoughtfully copyedited the entire book. Finally, we express our gratitude to our children and their spouses for bearing with us throughout—and for holding their tongues when they doubted that joint authorship of a book was good for a marriage. In fact, it was. And we hope that is yet another important lesson of this project.

Sarah V. Mackenzie
G. Calvin Mackenzie
Bowdoinham, Maine
June 2009

Acknowledgments

We gratefully acknowledge students and friends who supplied ideas for cases, helped us tease out the issues in particularly thorny cases or read parts of the manuscript and gave valuable feedback: Randi Arsenault, Pam Astbury, Andrew Bayer, Cindy Dean, Janet Fairman, Robert Griffin, Martha Kempe, Edie Kilgour, Rebecca Knight, Karen Larsen, Richard Lindsay, Sylvia Norton, Jonathan Moody, Susie Nybell, Gloria Smith, Tim Surrette, Terry Tibbetts, Rachelle Tome, Deborah Vose, Dan Welch, Todd West, and Terry Young.

Publisher's Acknowledgments

Corwin gratefully acknowledges the contributions of the following individuals:

James Anderson, Principal
Canaseraga Central School District, Canaseraga, NY

Patricia Bowman, Retired Principal and Educational Consultant
Inglewood, CA

Betty Brandenburg Yundt, Sixth-Grade Teacher and Curriculum
   Coordinator
Walker Intermediate School, Fort Knox, KY

Kathleen Choma, Statistics Teacher
South Brunswick High School, Marlboro, NJ

Julie Frederick, Kindergarten Teacher and Grade Level Expectation
    Alignment Teacher Leader
Viewlands Elementary School/Seattle Public Schools, Seattle, WA

Linda Irvin, Fourth-Grade Teacher
Sunflower Elementary School, Paola, KS

Sharon Jefferies, Third-Grade Teacher
Lakeville Elementary School, Orlando, FL

Loukea Kovanis-Wilson, Chemistry Teacher
Clarkston High School, Fenton, MI

About the Authors

 **Sarah V. Mackenzie** is associate professor of educational leadership at the University of Maine. She has dealt with the issues examined here for many years, first in her own hands-on experiences as a teacher and teacher leader and now in her role as a professor of educational leadership. Her most recent book, *Uncovering Teacher Leadership: Essays and Voices From the Field* (Corwin, 2007; coedited with Richard Ackerman), is a compilation of writing focused on the inner lives of teacher leaders. They published an article in the May 2006 issue of *Educational Leadership* titled "Uncovering Teacher Leadership."

In all of her work—as a teacher and a teacher of teachers and leaders—she has recognized the critical relationship between what teachers believe about their work and how successfully they perform that work. This book focuses sharp attention on that connection and offers abundant, practical aid to teachers and teacher leaders in fostering ethical leadership successfully in their own work lives and their own schools.

 **G. Calvin Mackenzie** is the Goldfarb Family Distinguished Professor of American Government at Colby College. He has written extensively about ethics in government and has led ethics seminars for public officials across the country. He served as chair of the Maine Commission on Governmental Ethics and Election Practices and was elected a fellow of the National Academy of Public Administration. A political scientist by training, Mackenzie has been a government professor and scholar for more than

30 years. He has written or edited 15 books, including a leading introductory American government text and several award-winning empirical studies of the national government. His latest book, *The Liberal Hour: Washington and the Politics of Change in the 1960s* (with Robert Weisbrot), was a finalist for the 2009 Pulitzer Prize in history.

PART I

Thinking About Ethics

To care for anyone else enough to make their problems one's own is ever the beginning of one's real ethical development.

—Felix Adler

1

Engaging in Ethics

> *Tina, a third-grade teacher in your school, cleaned out her attic and decided it was time to throw out cancelled checks from five years ago. She didn't have or feel she needed a paper shredder at home, so she brought her checks and some other documents to school and used the special education office paper shredder after school one day. You encounter her at this task. What do you do?*
>
> *Your school system is deliberating a pay-to-play policy for its athletic teams. You are an elementary teacher, so you have no close connection to the middle and high school students who might be involved. However, the concept offends your sense of fairness to students. If a school system deems a particular activity important enough to be part of its co-curricular program, shouldn't the system foot the bill? Shouldn't the system look at other ways to save money, e.g., having fewer teams if all teams cannot be supported, rather than impose a fee for participation on all the students who wish to play? Should you make your views known even if, technically, the policy does not affect you or your students?*

Schools are among the most complex institutions in our society. The relationships and interactions that unfold within their walls raise a ceaseless array of ethical questions and concerns. Teachers especially are confronted at nearly every turn with tasks or opportunities that have ethical implications. There is no escape from the constant need to recognize and do the right thing.

Fortunately, most of us do not enter this ethical thicket unarmed. We have been raised and nurtured by parents, mentors, and educators who helped us recognize the importance of ethical propriety, who taught us to see the difference between right and wrong, and placed a high value on the former. As adults in a learning environment, we have also come to know that we are role models, that our ethical choices have implications not just for ourselves but also for the students who watch us closely. This imposes a special kind of caution: the desire to be certain we're doing the right thing before we act. "Nothing is so conducive to good behavior," Dr. Johnson is reported to have said, "as the knowledge one is being watched." And in schools, we are always being watched.

But the training we bring and the care we take often are not enough to ensure that ethical propriety infuses all that we do. School settings are full of potential pitfalls and dilemmas that challenge even our best efforts to act ethically. Often, the problem is that we don't realize the ethical implications of an interaction. Sometimes we're tempted to minimize or distort those implications or subjugate them to convenience or self-interest. And occasionally, we confront an ethical dilemma that is too complex for us to respond with any certainty that we have made the right choice.

This book is not a bible. It does not offer eternal truths and lessons, the adoption of which guarantee ethical behavior. It is instead a guidebook, designed to help teachers through the maze of ethical challenges that are an inevitable part of their professional lives. We will try to identify the most common of those challenges and the kinds of situations in which they most often occur. We will offer some bedrock principles of ethical behavior and suggest ways in which they can be usefully applied to practical situations. And throughout we will provide the voices of teachers, explaining the real-world situations they have confronted, and then describe the processes of thought and action they employed in navigating through them.

Honing one's ethical sensitivities is a constant work in progress. There is something new to learn every day. Reading this book will not complete that process, but we hope it will help to facilitate, perhaps to accelerate it.

We will focus special attention on the role we feel teachers and administrators must take on as they help each other confront thorny issues. All educators face a dual task in their schools. In the first instance, they must cultivate their own sense of ethical propriety, because they are leaders and guides. By their own actions—and the perception of them—they set the standards for their schools. The ethical culture of any school is defined in large part by the norms that its members establish for their own behavior. Whatever they may preach will matter little if it is contradicted by the ways they act.

Commitment to high ethical standards by educators is the *sine qua non* of a sound ethical culture in any school.

Educators also have a responsibility to guide their colleagues on ethical behavior and ethical decision making. Formal efforts to introduce discussions of ethics into the meetings and routine conversations that take place among teachers are part of this obligation (Keith-Spiegel, Whitley, Balogh, Perkins, & Wittig, 2002). Informal efforts may involve simply asking questions about policies the school adopts or its method of implementation. Such questions, too, need to be routinely asked of oneself: "Does this action or policy conflict with my own moral compass? Will it be fair to everyone? What if there are exceptions to its implementation? Who decides?" Equally important is the careful construction of procedures and habits that allow teachers to seek and find help when they confront difficult ethical dilemmas. And essential as well for teachers is communicating with colleagues and administrators who may have failed to recognize an ethical challenge or to respond properly to it.

Creating a positive ethical environment in any institution, but in schools especially, depends above all else on communication (Enomoto & Kramer, 2007). In the pages that follow, we will offer many cases from the real world experience of teachers who have shared them with us. The range of complex situations in which they have found themselves is wide and evocative. But it only scratches the surface. Every reader of this book will have confronted situations of his or her own that do not precisely fit any of those discussed here, that raise ethical questions that cannot be answered in the same way they were answered here. The fabric of ethical principles and guidelines we will offer is far too thin to be stretched comfortably over every kind of ethical situation that arises in schools. It is essential, therefore, not to enter an ethical quagmire unaccompanied.

The best advice we can give anyone for effectively confronting an ethical challenge is to seek wise counsel before acting. Find someone whose independent judgment is reliable, who has no direct stake in the immediate situation, and solicit his or her guidance on how to act. We hope the lessons in the following pages help to shape those conversations, but they can never be a substitute for them.

Ethical Challenges in Schools

While the ethical issues that arise in school environments range widely, most fall within a few broad categories. We will identify those here and outline their parameters. In later chapters, we will discuss at length the role that teachers can play in dealing with these issues

Obeying the Law

This may seem the easiest of all moral principles—teachers should obey the law. The law is often made by adults with too little understanding of the young people to whom it applies, its effect on the learning process, or the impact it might have on the operation of a school. That one should obey the law is a good first response to any ethical dilemma. But there will be times in every educator's life when obeying the law does not seem to be the best way to respond to a complex situation.

In some states, for example, the law holds that when a person who is 18 has sexual relations with a person who is 15, a criminal act has occurred. But a typical high school has people of both ages and sometimes they engage in sexual relations. If a teacher learns of such a relationship, is it in the best interests of the students to report that knowledge to law enforcement officials?

In some states as well, teachers are required to report cases of abuse of children by a parent or someone else in their households. But the definition of abuse is often cloudy, and individual teachers may vary widely in their interpretation of its meaning.

One of the most common ethical dilemmas faced by any teacher is the discovery that a colleague or supervisor has done something unlawful. Should it be reported? Should it be reported that the school superintendent awarded the big paint job to a company owned by his brother-in-law? Should it be reported that a teacher is driving to school each day despite a suspended driver's license? Should it be reported that a colleague doesn't actually reside in the county where her school is located even though state law requires that?

Conflict of Interest

Each of us faces moments in our lives when our personal self-interest conflicts with our professional responsibilities. The potential for this kind of conflict of interest is present in virtually every job situation. A mentor teacher faces it when assessing a young probationary teacher who is her son's fiancée, or a teacher deals with potential conflict when serving on a committee to choose new computer hardware for the school where he teaches while owning stock in one of the bidding companies. Or consider the not uncommon problem of teaching in a school that your own child attends. Should that child be assigned to your classes? Should you be in a position of leading or supervising other teachers who have your child in their classes? Should you broach your concerns with her teacher when you think your child has been unfairly evaluated on a term paper? In situations like this, the conflicts between one's roles of teacher and parent are unending and very much in need of attention and constraint.

A common response by those possessed of a potential conflict of interest is to declare that they won't be affected by it. "Don't worry," they may say. "I'll vote to adopt the best computer hardware for the school even if it's not sold by the company in which I hold stock." Or, "I can assess that new teacher objectively even if she is going to marry my son." Perhaps so, but who will ever believe that if the action that follows serves the actor's self-interest? In creating an ethical environment in a school, perceptions matter deeply. One can be sure, for example, that if a teacher were to participate in the hardware selection described here, and the committee's decision was to adopt the hardware sold by the company in which that teacher owned stock, the losing bidder would cry foul and suggest that the choice was infected by conflict of interest. Whatever the reality, the appearance of a conflict of interest would prevail.

The only reliable cure in situations such as this is for people who possess a potential conflict of interest to declare it and to remove themselves from the decision making in which it might affect their judgment. That is not always easy, but it is always necessary. Every school committed to high ethical standards needs to have a policy that defines conflicts of interest and indicates the steps that should always be taken to avoid them.

Misuse or Abuse of Position

In our work lives, we are often afforded opportunities to do things or to use equipment that may benefit us personally. Our schools often possess things that we do not own or have in our homes: photocopiers, video cameras or projectors, laptop computers, lawnmowers, and the like. There may be times when it would be a significant personal convenience to use the school's equipment for personal purposes that are unrelated to the task of the school. The video camera that was purchased to record school athletic contests would be perfect for videotaping our cousin's wedding. Or the custodian's commercial vacuum cleaner might be very helpful in cleaning up the garage at home this weekend. Or I could copy my income tax return on the school's photocopier or take home a ream of that printer paper from the supply closet for my printer at home.

The convenience and low cost of using school equipment for non-school purposes are highly tempting and most of us have succumbed to those temptations from time to time. But it is wrong. We may convince ourselves that there is no cost to the school when we borrow its equipment, but that is a delusion, and it wouldn't matter even if it were true.

"No harm, no foul" may be the rule in basketball, but not in ethics. Materials and equipment purchased for school purposes should not be used for individual purposes unrelated to the school. This is true in any school setting, but in public schools there is the added dimension of the equipment in question being purchased with taxpayer funds. How often do we read about scandals in which public officials abuse their access to cars or staff or office allowances to transport their spouses on shopping trips or to go on official trips that are actually vacations? These all represent abuse of position, and they differ only in degree from the teacher who uses the school video camera for a family wedding.

What are the limits in the use of the school photocopier? What about exchanging personal e-mails or making online purchases on school computers during the school day? Are there ever conditions when a school lawnmower can be used on a teacher's lawn, say with the payment of a rental fee to the school? Even though they sometimes seem to deal with incidental costs, these are important questions because they broach the larger issue of misuse of one's position. It is important for teachers and their schools to recognize the potential threats here to the ethical culture of their work environment and to establish clear policies to guide those who wish to act ethically and those who might be tempted to do otherwise.

Representation of Individual Clients

The recent rapid expansion in private tutoring, private classes, and college counseling has raised a new set of ethical challenges to schools. Suppose a parent of a student you're currently teaching comes to you and says, "You've done a wonderful job of teaching our son; he's never been so excited about learning. We'd like to hire you to tutor him on Saturday mornings so that he'll do well when he takes his college entrance exams. We'll pay you $50 an hour for three hours each Saturday." How do you respond?

Here we see at least two principles in conflict, the classic ethical dilemma. One is the understanding that teachers are free to use their off-duty time as they wish, including engaging in activities that allow them to supplement their teaching salaries. If you want to paint houses or work at the local hardware store or drive a cab, you should be free to do that as long as it is on your own time.

But what if what you would like to do on your own time intersects with your teaching responsibilities? If you accept the invitation to tutor a student in your classes, you must understand that other students, and their parents, may see this through a different set of lenses. To them, this may be little more than an effort by the parents to bribe you to give their son favorable treatment in school. It will be hard for you to convince objective observers that your judgment of that student's work is unaffected by the money his parents are paying you each week. There is a clear conflict here between your right to enhance your income on your own time and the school's need to maintain an ethical climate in which fair and equitable treatment of all students is paramount.

Representation of individual clients might occur in another way. Suppose a textbook publisher approaches you at a statewide conference and invites you to come to a presentation the company is giving a few weeks later. The presentation is for teachers nominated by their principals and will be held at a local resort where you will be provided meals and overnight accommodations. You're invited as well to bring your spouse or partner. The publisher indicates that it is an opportunity to introduce you to some new texts and their authors. You agree to participate, and at the presentation you are told that if you are impressed with these new texts and if your school adopts any of them, you will receive a voucher for a three-day weekend with your family at this resort.

Back at school, you meet with teachers in your department or grade level to discuss the selection of new texts for the following year. What obligations, if any, do you have with regard to your relationship with this publisher? Here it is important to see that you have become, at least potentially, a representative of this publisher. An exchange relationship has been established: you have been offered something of value (the three-day weekend at the resort) in exchange for your efforts to secure the adoption of the publisher's books. While you did nothing wrong by attending the presentation, you tread on very shaky ethical ground if you participate in the selection of new texts without fully disclosing your relationship with the publisher.

Teachers can play a valuable role in each of these situations by helping their schools develop policies to guide all teachers when confronted with opportunities like this to take on clients or become agents for financial reward. Then when parents offer private tutoring opportunities or publishers create financial incentives for adopting their books, teachers will have a much clearer sense (1) that there are ethical issues at stake and (2) that a proper response should be guided by established policies. Perhaps it is acceptable to tutor a student in your school as long as that student is not enrolled in your classes. Or perhaps it is acceptable to attend the publisher's presentation as long as no remuneration is received if its books are adopted. Only when clear borders are drawn in school policies can teachers be certain that they have not sunk into an ethical swamp.

Nonschool Employment or Business

Many school employees supplement their salaries by engaging in other employment or owning businesses. Relatively low teacher salaries make this necessary and the number of days when they are not obligated to be in school makes this possible for many teachers. But keeping school employment separate from nonschool employment is a constant challenge, a central concern in maintaining the healthy ethical culture of a school.

Nonschool employment should take place outside the school; it should not impose on any school resources, facilities, or equipment; and it should not prevent teachers from being prepared and properly rested for their school responsibilities. Nor should nonschool employment be in occupations that undermine the reputation of school or the teaching profession generally or the respect that either should expect in their communities.

Consider these possibilities. A teacher owns an auction business and makes and receives auction-related phone calls at school during the day. A teacher uses school photocopiers to reproduce brochures for her scrapbooking business. A teacher makes a profit from buying and selling camera equipment on eBay and uses the computer in the teachers' lounge to enter bids between classes. Each of these raises common questions about the line between on-duty and off-duty obligations and constraints. And in an era when e-mail, cell phones, and BlackBerries facilitate communication anywhere any time, the challenge is much greater than it was when there was one telephone per school under the watchful eye of the school secretary in the main office.

What about a teacher who works as a bouncer on weekends at a seedy local bar? Or the teacher who works in the summer for a company that manufactures performance-enhancing drugs which, though legal, have been banned for athletes at his school? As these examples suggest, ethical complexity grows when we try to define the line of propriety that separates teachers' obligations to their schools from the freedom to do on their own time what any other citizen is permitted to do.

Memberships and Affiliations

Freedom of association is a right guaranteed by the U.S. Constitution. It is a treasured American value. But the exercise of this right can be a complication when we think about educators in public schools. Although they may stand for wide tolerance and intellectual openness, schools are not value-free. On some matters, inevitably, schools will have an institutional valence. School missions may profess the equality of males and females and of people of different races and religions. However, if the communities they serve are divided on certain values, educational leaders may wish to avoid taking institutional positions on controversial issues such as abortion or gay marriage.

The problem comes when teachers or other school employees join groups that have values or views at odds with those of the school. A teacher may be a member of a church that defines abortion or homosexuality as sins. Perhaps the soccer coach is a member of a local club that denies membership to women. An educational technician may be a leader in the local chapter of Aryan Nation, a group that opposes the mixing of the races.

The moral high ground is often hard to define in cases like these. It is easy enough for schools to require that employees park their personal beliefs—especially those that conflict with prominent school values—at the front door. But can a moral person have one set of values in school and another on the outside? And how far can a school legitimately go in circumscribing the impact of employee memberships and affiliations if individuals have a constitutional right to them?

Civility

One of the categories of ethical behavior least discussed is the conduct of interpersonal relations. We tend not to think of this as an "ethical" concern. But there is little that defines our moral credentials more than the way we treat other people.

Schools are places of close and intense personal relationships. How we handle these relationships—how fair-minded we are, how tolerant, how discreet, and how cordial—are all measures of the values we bring to our work. Contextualizing our personal desires and self-interests by juxtaposing them and, when necessary, subordinating them to the greater needs of the school is the essence of moral behavior.

We may have little admiration for the teaching skills or commitment of the colleague who is nearing retirement and appears "burned out." We may find it difficult to converse, perhaps even to be in the same room, with the colleague who criticizes every decision made by the principal. We may have been angered when we overheard two female students talking about the leering looks they thought they were receiving from a male teacher. Perhaps the short skirts and revealing blouses worn by the new social studies teacher seem inappropriate school dress. How we handle these feelings and how our handling of them contributes to the work climate in our schools are important components of our ethical obligations to each other and to the school community.

Nowhere is this more evident, nor more potentially corrosive, than in the ways we talk about our colleagues. Since humans seem to have an enduring fascination with other people's lives, schools are places where gossip is rife. Gossip can be harmless and fun, as when we wonder whether a colleague is expecting a baby or likely to start a doctoral program. But gossip can also be mean, vindictive, and damaging. Controlling the urge to trespass too deeply into matters that are none of our business or to cast aspersions on colleagues who are not there to defend themselves is essential to civility. And civility is the essence of a healthy ethical climate in any school (Palmer, 2007; Sizer & Sizer, 1999).

Role Models

Like Caesar's wife, teachers are highly visible figures and must be "above suspicion." While no one can properly argue that invisibility is a justification for unethical behavior—it's okay as long as it's not seen—one can certainly argue that those who work in the public eye have to be especially careful in their ethical decision making because their actions will be judged by a critical audience. The impact of that is especially acute for teachers who will be judged by young people looking for role models for their own behaviors.

Jackson, Boostrom, and Hansen's (1998) research helps experienced teachers remember that we teach who we are. Learning is not just the transmission of information and inspiration about intellectual substance, it is also the impression that adults make on children and adolescents. We should be fair and tolerant in our interactions and seek to do the right thing in our behavior because those are important ethical standards. But we should seek to meet those standards as well because they provide clear and good lessons to the students who watch and copy us closely.

The teachers who are guilty of rowdy fan behavior at sports contests, who lie when asked a question they can't answer, who take a sick day to go to the beach—in all of these actions, they teach who they are. And the lessons can inhibit the ethical growth of their students and undermine the ethical culture of their schools. All of the situations we explore in this book get back to the students: What are they learning and what should they be learning as these significant adults in their lives wrestle with dilemmas that invariably have to do with what is the right and just behavior? These people, their teachers, have the important job of shaping future generations, academically, of course, but also socially and ethically.

In the next chapter, we provide some overarching principles that can help teachers think through situations so they are better prepared to act according to a clear ethical code when they are confronted with difficult choices. In the subsequent chapters, we take a look at ethical questions that may arise in teachers' work lives as they interact with different people in their school communities. Although each chapter focuses on a particular relationship, the issues are complex and usually involve other people from different groups and invariably resonate with the notion that we teach who we are. Children, however, are the bottom line.

2

Ethical Behavior

Some General Principles

Ethical behavior has two central elements. The first is to recognize an ethical dilemma or challenge when one occurs. The second is to discern and undertake the right action in such a situation (Enomoto & Kramer, 2007; Strike, 2007).

The human experience has yielded some sturdy principles for identifying and responding to ethical situations. These are not always adequate to resolve fully the dilemmas we face, but they are useful aids for navigating rough ethical seas. In combination with the earlier caveat to seek good counsel, they can help to narrow the focus and limn out the key concerns whenever an ethical challenge is confronted.

The Golden Rule

A good starting point in any ethical consideration is to ask: How would I want to be treated in this situation? At a minimum, you would want your opinion respected, you would want to be listened to, you would not want to be deceived or cheated. So you act toward others as you want them to act toward you.

Mutual respect is the best possible lubricant for any set of personal interactions in any institutional setting. We may differ from each other in many ways, but we are all equal in one important way—as moral agents. Each of us in our persons and in our ideas and beliefs deserves respect and is obligated to grant that respect to others (Barth, 2001; Tschannen-Moran, 2004). We don't have to agree with others' views or beliefs or admire them or the ways they behave; nevertheless, we have to treat people with genuine respect, courtesy, and decency. Only then can we expect the same treatment in return.

A teacher in your school may be a member of a church that engages in rituals that seem to you, well, weird. You are under no obligation to view these practices otherwise. As a person of curious intellect, though, you may want to learn more about them, their derivation and meaning within the theology of that faith. But you owe the teacher who practices that faith the same respect you would want from him with regard to your own practice or nonpractice of religion.

On an even more practical level, the golden rule can help us deal with some of the most unpleasant aspects of our work roles, particularly those of us who have supervisory responsibilities, whether formal or informal. If our own work were unsatisfactory to our supervisors and we were at risk of negative job performance, we would want to be told that at the earliest possible time and given explicit substantive explanations of the concerns. We would want the opportunity to respond and, where necessary, to adjust our performance to meet expectations. Teachers and administrators owe that same kind of regard to those whom they supervise and evaluate: early warning of concerns, substantive detail, and ample opportunity for correction. When considering how best to deal with difficult situations like this, it is helpful to consider how one would want to be treated if the roles were reversed.

Helpful as it is in shaping interpersonal relationships, the golden rule is not adequate guidance for every kind of moral quandary. Hence, some other decision rules emerge to fill in the gaps.

Rule of Benevolence

The rule of benevolence is sometimes referred to as the utilitarian principle and has been most fully discussed in the philosophies of Jeremy Bentham and John Stuart Mill. This rule holds that one should act in ways that conduce to the greatest good for the greatest number or the least harm to the greatest number.

As we know, many ethical situations involve conflicts between two principles, each of which have some value (Berlak & Berlak, 1981; Enomoto & Kramer, 2007; Kidder, 2003). One way to choose among them is to try to determine which will provide the greatest good or least harm to the largest number. When President Truman confronted one of the great moral dilemmas of human history—whether or not to use the atomic bomb against Japan in 1945—he relied heavily, though not explicitly, on this rule. His advisors indicated that the loss of civilian life in Japan would be unprecedented if the bomb were used; tens of thousands might die. But they also warned that if the bomb were not used to end the war and an invasion of the home islands of Japan took place, the number of casualties of both Americans and Japanese would be much larger. He chose the path that promised the least harm to the largest number.

Fortunately teachers and school leaders face no decisions with consequences as large as that. But they do face situations, often with significant ethical implications, where weighing one valid principle or one desirable outcome against another is essential. The application of affirmative action policies is an example.

When affirmative action programs were initiated in the second half of the twentieth century, many school systems were forced to confront lengthy histories of segregating both students and teachers by race and denying certain jobs and equal salaries to women. To compensate, school systems began to accelerate their hiring of minority teachers in schools that had few or none from minority groups in the past, and they began to give women opportunities to catch up with men. In practice, this often meant that a qualified minority candidate was hired or promoted even though there were white candidates who appeared to have superior qualifications.

White or male candidates who did not get jobs or promotions for which they were most qualified and which they felt they deserved thought that such policies imposed significant sacrifices on them. They often felt they were being treated unfairly and some called this "reverse discrimination." There was little denying their feelings or their claims.

The justification for these affirmative action policies was that they produced the most good for the most people. While some individuals suffered by not getting jobs or promotions, a much larger number was welcomed into the mainstream, given opportunities to participate fully in the lives of their communities, and afforded some compensation for generations of discrimination and abuse. Minority children and girls had teachers, administrators, coaches, and role models of their own race or gender.

Affirmative action has often been unpopular because it seems to violate deeply held principles of fair play: That one should be judged on his or her merits alone. But that had not been the case historically in many places, and utilitarian principles were applied to try to compensate for those past violations.

Rule of Universality

The rule of universality is a simple and often very helpful way to reflect on our personal behavior: Would it be acceptable if everyone did it? One of the easiest ways to convince ourselves that our own actions are not unethical is by minimizing their impact. Say we are driving along a country road, we finish the banana we have been eating, and we toss the peel out the window. No problem, we tell ourselves; traffic is light out here, there is no one around, it will not hurt anything. Or we are leaving school for the weekend and realize we forgot to stop at the mall to buy more paper for the printer at home. And our spouse specifically asked for this in order to print out the garden club newsletter. So we go to the school supply closet and grab a couple of reams of paper. It is not a big deal, we tell ourselves; there are dozens of boxes of paper in there; no one will miss it.

But what if everyone did it? Would it be acceptable if every teacher in the school stopped at the supply closet on Friday afternoon to stock up on supplies for personal or family use over the weekend? We should judge our behavior not by its magnitude but by its propriety. If it is wrong, it is wrong in small doses as well as large. Whenever we start to excuse our behavior by saying, "Just this once," or "I'll make an exception in this case," or "It is a trivial amount," what we are doing is suspending the rules of good behavior. And whenever we do that, unethical behavior is likely to follow.

The rule of universality requires us to universalize our potential actions before we undertake them, to judge their propriety by universal standards applicable to everyone, not to treat our choices as exceptional or insignificant. Unethical behavior often takes place because it is more convenient than acting ethically. Going to the school supply closet for paper is more convenient, for example, than making an extra trip to the mall. But convenience should not be a justification for improper behavior. Universalizing one's behavior before acting is a helpful way to avoid poor judgment.

Rule of Publicity

Another way in which we sometimes try to excuse our unethical behavior is by convincing ourselves that no one will notice. It is unlikely we would even contemplate taking that paper from the supply closet if we had to explain to the school secretary that we are taking paper that belongs to the school for personal use at home.

But if we can just walk into the closet unseen and walk out with the paper, somehow it does not seem so wrong.

The rule of publicity is intended as an antidote to this. It asks: Would it be acceptable behavior if everyone knew about it? Sometimes this is called a "smell test," as in "that kind of explanation would not survive a simple smell test." And sometimes it is called the "kid on your shoulder" rule: Would you do it if your own child were sitting on your shoulder watching you?

Any action that seems acceptable only when accomplished in secret should always give us pause. Suppose, for example, it is a beautiful late spring day, and you call the principal saying you do not feel well and are going to take a sick day. Then you spend the day in the sun by the pool. Would you do that if everyone knew that is what you were doing? Would you regard that as acceptable behavior if your local town manager did that? Would you be comfortable explaining to your children that you lied to your supervisor and took a sick day when you were not sick?

In this age of electronic communication, remembering this principle can be helpful in avoiding the potential embarrassment and problematic outcome of writing something negative about a colleague, student, or supervisor and having what you wrote end up in the wrong hands. The fear of publicity can and should have a chilling effect on our communications as there are obviously things we write and say that are not meant for public consumption. The rule of publicity should be cautionary, too. The critical e-mail about a colleague might well be forwarded to persons for whom it was not intended, including the person about whom it was written. Before sending off such an e-mail, it might be useful to ask yourself: Would I be comfortable if many people saw this? Sometimes, when it is necessary to make comments or pass judgments about colleagues, it is best to do it orally, to avoid the risk of the endlessly circulating e-mail.

Think about this as well in terms of your public behavior and speech. So much that happens today is recorded by someone. History simply does not evaporate as it once did. Years ago if you went to a holiday party for teachers, had too much to drink, and danced seductively with a colleague, people might have laughed about it at school the next day, but there was no record of it and the memory soon faded. These days, people at the party probably have cell phones capable of recording video. Someone might record your dancing and think it so entertaining (or wrong) that he uploads the video to YouTube. Now 100,000 people have seen it and, as Desi used to say to Lucy, you've got "some 'splainin' to do." The rule of publicity could have saved you lots of embarrassment; even more, it might have prevented all those questions about whether you were a fit role model for young people.

Think of these rules as a checklist for ethical behavior. No one of them alone is likely to resolve every potential ethical quandary. But if you confront a situation that may have ethical implications, a situation in which you want to do the right thing, ask yourself how would you want to be treated by others, what action produces the greatest good for the largest number, would it be okay if everyone did what I am contemplating doing, would my action stand wide scrutiny? The answers to those questions should provide a reliable foundation of ethical certainty for the action you decide to take.

The Problem of Specifics

Principles are valuable, but often too abstract. The ethical challenges we confront in our work lives are often complicated by practical realities that make the application of sound ethical principles more difficult than they seem when we read them in a book like this. The devil, as we know, is in the details.

A common complicating factor is that our self-interest is often at odds with good ethical behavior. Take the case of the coach whose star player misbehaves badly. He knows that the behavior must be punished in some way, but he also wants to win games. Suspending the player or even removing him from the team may be the best way to underscore standards of proper behavior, but it will probably cost the team some victories and may even put the coach's job in jeopardy if he is not successful at winning.

Self-interest intervenes most often in our calculation of whether it is wise to report the unethical behavior of a colleague or supervisor. Suppose you have been a teacher for several years and decide you would like to try your hand at administration. You know the assistant principal in your school is retiring in another year and you think you might apply for the job when she does. You have been taking some courses to be sure you qualify for the job when it becomes vacant. Today, however, you overhear a conversation that makes you wonder about its potential impact on your future. You are eating with your spouse at a local restaurant and overhear voices from the next booth. You cannot see or be seen, but you recognize the voice of your school's principal. He is describing to someone how he has dealt with the summer's hot weather. He explains that he ordered air conditioners for several of the rooms at school, but he made sure to order three more air conditioners than were needed and took those to use in his house. He adds that principals are underpaid, and there are a few "perks" of the job that help to compensate for that. Just having this knowledge is problematic, but contemplating applying for an administrative position adds even more complexity.

The principal is guilty of misusing school funds, and there is no question the principal has acted unethically. We will discuss in greater detail later in the book how one might respond to such knowledge. Suffice it to note that situations like this—where self-interest conflicts with ethical responsibility—are a common reason why acting ethically is often more than just a matter of recognizing an ethical principle and applying it.

Another one of these complicating factors is incomplete information. You may have some reason to believe that an employee in your school has done something wrong, but you are not certain. Even if the potential violation is significant, you wonder is you should report it, perhaps risking the job or career of the alleged perpetrator, before you have complete certainty that your information is full and accurate.

Knowing part of a story or hearsay is a frequent concern in matters involving improper relationships between teachers and students. If a student comes to you and says she thinks you ought to know that one of her classmates has been meeting one of your teaching colleagues at a local park in the evenings and "it's not to talk about homework," what should your response be? Again, we'll discuss such situations later, but we note here the burden of uncertainty. If the allegation is true, this is a deeply troubling situation. But is the allegation true? What obligation do you have, if any, to pursue this? Uncertainty often keeps us from acting, from speaking up. Should it?

Very often ethical principles conflict in very complex situations. School leaders sometimes find themselves caught in a dilemma when a teacher is found to have acted improperly. On the one hand, it may seem desirable to punish the offender in some public way that will send a clear message to others who work at the school and perhaps even convey to the community that the school takes its obligations seriously and imposes high standards on its employees. On the other hand, publicizing the misbehavior and the punishment may jeopardize the school's standing in the community just when new contract negotiations are under way or a bond issue is on the ballot to construct a new elementary school. Bad news about a single teacher's behavior may be enough to tip the political balance against the broader interests of the community. One could argue that publicity about the action and the school's response is the right ethical course here, an application of the rule of publicity described above. But one could also argue that the broader interests of the community and its children in getting the new school that is desperately needed outweigh the value of publicizing this case, an application of the utilitarian principle of the greatest good for the largest number.

Perhaps more than any other cause for difficulty in applying ethical principles is the unwillingness to recognize that any ethical principle is at stake or, if one is recognized, to minimize its significance. "No one will notice." "Everybody does it." "It's not illegal." "Nobody ever got in trouble for this." "The union will back us up if anybody questions it." "It's not costing anybody anything." We have all heard some or all of these excuses for bending the rules, for circumventing ethical propriety, even for breaking the law. Convenience, self-interest, laziness, disdain—all of these are convenient and far-too-common deterrents to ethical behavior.

Add to these factors the business we are in. We are keepers of the public's trust in so many ways, not least of which is that we are entrusted with the education of children. We represent the school in our outside activities; inside the school every move is scrutinized. We do our work in the interpersonal realm constantly rubbing up against others' interests, needs, and feelings (Ayers, 2004; Sizer & Sizer, 1999; Sockett, 1990; Tschannen-Moran, 2004). So while we must be clear about our beliefs and our ethical principles, we have to consider the people around us who are affected and influenced by our actions. Complications indeed.

What Lies Ahead

This book is a practical primer on ethical behavior in schools. It focuses on the responsibilities of teachers, teacher leaders—both formal and informal—and administrators. The book is organized concentrically with teachers at the center of relationships common to all schools. We begin with students and their parents, then colleagues, then supervisors and the community. In each section, we pay primary attention to the task and difficulty of managing those relationships to ensure the creation and maintenance of a healthy ethical culture in a school.

The principles and problems we have discussed here will show up again in the pages that follow, often in the form of cases drawn from the real experiences of the scores of teachers we have consulted in researching this book and who have been so generous in sharing with us their tales from the front lines. Our job is to draw useful lessons from those experiences and to explain them in ways that will help readers navigate the challenges they are sure to face in their own schools.

PART II

Acting Ethically: Teachers and Their Constituents

The best way to teach morality is to make it a habit with children.

—Aristotle

3

The Essential Learning Relationship

Teachers and Students

T he central relationship in any school is the one between teacher and student. Teachers teach and students learn. But, of course, it is never that simple. Teachers do not just teach, and students do not just learn. There are many teachers and many students in a school, yet they are surrounded by colleagues, parents, administrators, coaches, guidance counselors, and a wide variety of other people who affect and constrain the essential bond between students and teachers.

The ethical concerns that arise in the relationship between teachers and students often involve other people. Teachers may be pressured to shape or direct their connection with a student in order to meet the needs or desires of some third party. In those commonly occurring situations, teachers find themselves juggling their obligations to a student with other relationships in the school and community. It is not simple to find the right balance—or to do the right thing.

The right thing, most teachers would agree, is to do what is in the long-term best interests of the student. But even that can be difficult to determine; the short term and long term are sometimes in conflict, as the following case suggests.

FOR THE GOOD OF THE TEAM

Joan was troubled when Michael came to see her. A junior in one of her English classes, Michael had not been performing well lately. In fact, he had been absent for the past few days and had not submitted several writing assignments. As required by school policy, Joan needed to send his name to the athletic director because he was a basketball player not passing at the mid-quarter mark. Under that same policy, the athletic director would be obligated to remove Michael from the team at least until the next marking period at the end of the quarter. By then, the basketball season would be over. The only way for Michael to continue playing would be for Joan to change his grade to passing and to withdraw the notification she had sent to the athletic director.

On the day the mid-quarter reports were due, Michael approached Joan just before the lunch break and sheepishly asked if he could talk to her. "Of course," she said. "What's going on?" Michael told her that he had been having a hard time lately because his mother had kicked him out of the house. They had argued about his work schedule at the grocery store interfering with his studies and with basketball practice. "That's why I have been behind in my work. I hope you understand that I really, really want to be able to play basketball. This is my junior year. I need to stay on the team, so that I have a chance at a scholarship next year. I just have a lot going on right now."

Joan wanted to be sympathetic. Michael was someone she worried about. He had potential, but he seemed to be unpredictable and unfocused. She knew his mother could also be described in the same terms. Joan had not realized how important basketball was to him until she heard his plea. "I really need to be on the team," he said. "They need me. I can't let the team down. If you'll say I'm passing, I'll make up all the work I missed. I promise."

Joan had been in this situation before. When she was younger, she had even changed a student's grade at the end of the year so she would be able to play soccer in the fall. Lately, though, she was more cautious. She had matured and was increasingly aware that what she did in her classroom had the potential to affect the whole school. She thought, too, about a student she had a few years ago who, when he was suspended from school and dropped from the basketball team for a "minor infraction," said he felt as if the rug had been pulled out from under him. "Teachers kept making deals with me," he had told her. "They let me get away with things. They didn't really care. I wasn't prepared for this punishment. They finally got sick of me. If they had cared, they would have been stricter from the beginning."

Joan knew Michael's home life was difficult, and she knew that basketball could be his ticket to college. Without a scholarship there was little chance his mother could afford tuition bills. Although she wanted to be supportive of Michael, she was also aware of her obligation to the school and its rules regarding extracurricular activities. She was also concerned about the long-term impact on Michael himself if she showed him he could circumvent the rules. And would he also see, ultimately, that she didn't care enough to hold him to a high standard of performance?

What should Joan to do?

Discussion

No teacher is an island. Because of the increasing emphasis on collegiality and collaboration in school, teachers have a heightened sense of responsibility for the whole school and for all the students there (Keith-Spiegal, Whitley, Balogh, Perkins, & Wittig, 2002; Sergiovanni, 1992). When they make decisions, they know they represent all their colleagues. Individual decisions accumulate into precedent and policy. So in sorting out conflicts like the ones described in this case, it is not enough merely to do what feels good or right in the immediate circumstances but to think more broadly about the impacts of a single decision on the school community.

While it is important for Joan to ask herself what is best for Michael, she must also ask what will best serve the goals and values of the school. And it is especially important that Joan understand that this is a public decision and not simply a secret deal between a teacher and a student. Her decision in this case has implications not just for Michael but for all students and all teachers in her school. In making complex decisions like this, teachers should be able to articulate their beliefs and rationales to the other stakeholders—students, certainly, but also parents and colleagues. Joan is obligated to be sensitive to the trust (Meier, 1995; Tschannen-Moran, 2004) that teachers must have for each other as they teach and function as members of a moderately interdependent group (Bandura, 1999; Sergiovanni, 1992).

Experienced teachers come to understand the role all teachers play in the lives of students. Whether they come to it instinctively or through a series of consciousness-raising critical events, they know they teach themselves (Jackson, Boostrom, & Hansen, 1998). Teachers are role models for students who closely watch their every move. Just as they mimic their parents, students pick up on the ethic of their teachers. Teachers cannot afford to underestimate this critical component of their responsibility to students (Sizer & Sizer, 1999).

So we return to the question, what should Joan do? As a starting point, she should take time to think through the options carefully and fully. An immediate decision in the midst of an emotional conversation is rarely necessary or wise. Joan's immediate response to Michael should be that she has followed the policies of the school, policies that were known to him when he allowed himself to fall into this predicament. But she should also note that she takes seriously his desire to make amends and that she will take his request under consideration and consult with others about it. She should make an appointment to discuss this further with him as soon as she has had more time to contemplate and consult.

Joan is confronted with what Rushworth Kidder (2003) calls a true ethical dilemma: when the decision maker considers two alternatives both of which she perceives to be "right." Joan initially sees her choice as between mercy or care on the one hand and justice on the other. Taking into consideration what she knows about Michael, Joan is inclined to be lenient. He is not a serial offender and has not asked for any kind of special treatment before. She had not realized how important basketball was to him, but now she does. He had been doing fairly well in her class until the last few weeks, and in other classes, he was getting by despite his problems at home. His grades were not affected in social studies and science because there had only been in-school tests, which he passed. His math teacher said he had never done homework consistently, but he always managed to pass the tests. Was Joan the only one, then, who would keep him from playing? Did it matter if she was?

One could also describe her dilemma in the paradigm of the individual versus the community. The community must function with rules and norms that everyone follows even if there are harmful consequences for a single individual. Think of the rule of universality described in Chapter 2. Would it be right for every teacher to bend the rules—as Michael has requested that she do here—for every athlete who wanted to continue to play on a team? This argument is particularly prevalent in schools where many teachers feel students must see equal consequences for any infraction because "rules are rules" and they must apply equally to all lest there be no communal order.

If Joan does decide to be merciful, what message does this send to the student about his role in the school community? Does it imply sports are more important than academics? That there are loopholes for hard luck cases? Or even just for people who ask? Does giving in to his request remove some of his burden of responsibility for his own actions—a burden that schools should help instill in students? Would she, in a way, be disrespectful of him as a student if she circumvented the rules?

Joan also has to think, too, of her role as a member of the faculty, as a professional and member of a particular community (Shapiro & Gross, 2008; Shapiro & Stepkovich, 2005). When the faculty recommended this strict extracurricular policy last year, Joan had misgivings and tried to convince fellow teachers that it could punish students who were on the borderline, students who were often hurt by stringent "zero-tolerance" policies like this. She was not successful in that effort, and the new policy was established despite her opposition. The majority of her colleagues saw it as a clear statement of the school's primary emphasis on academics. She is responsible for implementing that policy. In fact, as one who opposed the policy when it was under consideration, she bears a special responsibility to avoid placing her own beliefs and predispositions above those enacted into policy by the majority of her colleagues.

Having thought about the dilemma she faces and sought to sort out the implications of each of her options, Joan's next response should be to seek the advice of others. This is a step too often and too lightly avoided by teachers who trust their own judgments, who don't want students to view them as powerless to act alone or who don't want their autonomy as teachers constrained by colleagues or community norms. But consultation in a case like this serves two essential and valuable objectives.

First, it will help Joan make a prudent decision. Ultimately the choice is hers and she will be responsible for it. But by consulting with a trusted friend or with Michael's other teachers or with a faculty council, Joan will have opened up her decision making to a wider array of views and considerations than she is able to bring to it alone. Her decision should be better informed and more cautious as a result of this consultation.

Second, by consulting before deciding, Joan gains a measure of protection from those who might disagree with her ultimate choice. Suppose, for example, she decides to abide by the policy and Michael is forced to leave the basketball team. The coach may criticize Joan for not taking the student's personal situation into account and jeopardizing his future because of her insensitivity and inflexibility. But if she has consulted with others and followed a course that represents a consensus among them, she will have support in responding to the coach's criticisms. Even if there is no consensus among those with whom she consults or if she believes the right ethical choice here is one that does not follow the advice she receives from others, the act of consultation should give her a clearer sense of the parameters of the decision and more confidence in the propriety of the choice she makes. She can make a more effective defense of her decision because she has a more acute sense of the arguments on the other side.

Joan's primary ethical obligation in this case is to avoid secrecy or deceit. Whether she chooses to enforce the school's policy or to grant Michael's request for an exception because of his personal circumstances, she should be prepared to justify her choice to a larger audience than Michael alone. The rule of publicity is an important source of guidance here. She should take the action she would take if everyone—faculty colleagues, administrators, other students, and parents—knew about it.

The safest course for Joan in this case is to abide by the rules. She cannot be faulted for that, either procedurally or ethically. The rule of benevolence would generally support this approach because abiding by established policies normally ensures the greatest good for the greatest number: All students should be aware of the consequences of not passing their courses and should not be distracted by extracurricular activities from their academic work. Harmful as this may seem to Michael, it serves the purposes of the entire school community, and Michael's "punishment" may be an object lesson to others.

On the other hand, applying the golden rule might lead Joan to show mercy because that is what she would want if she were in Michael's position or if her own child was in a similar situation. If she decides that the right choice here is to give Michael another chance, perhaps by negotiating a deadline for completion of his unfinished assignments in exchange for temporarily altering his mid-quarter grade, Joan's ethical position is more tenuous. A heavy burden of justification falls on anyone who violates community standards or policies. If Joan believes this is the right course, then she is obligated to gather support from other teachers and to present the case for an exception to the faculty council, the school principal, or some other appropriate authoritative entity. If she can make that case successfully and an exception is formally granted, she has satisfied her ethical obligations. If she cannot, then her only proper recourse is to enforce the school's policies.

In the end, it is important to note the difference between violating a policy and seeking an exception to it. If Joan's immediate reaction to Michael had been a favorable response to his request, without thoughtful contemplation of its implications or proper consultation, her decision would have trespassed nearly all ethical boundaries. Enforcing the policy or seeking a justifiable exception to it through proper channels, on the other hand, would have trespassed none.

A NEW BALL GAME?

It was Pauline's first year as an assistant principal and she looked forward to her work at Pinewood Elementary in the community where her family had just moved. During her second month on the job, she began a series of class visitations and teacher observations. Knowing she would play a role in teacher evaluation, she immediately started to visit classrooms.

During one of these visitations in the room of Mr. Williams, a fourth-grade teacher, she was surprised when he threw a ball at a student who was not paying attention to the math problem he was solving on the board. The ball was soft and filled with cotton; the student was not hurt. But to Pauline, throwing a ball at a student was a violent act, and it troubled her.

At the end of the day, she decided to go to Mr. Williams's room to talk with him about his actions. It was not her intent to chastise him but rather to have a discussion about how such an act fit into his pedagogy—and perhaps to suggest that it had no place in the school for which she now had leadership responsibilities.

Williams had been teaching fourth graders at the school for more than 25 years and was nearing retirement. He welcomed Pauline to his room but cut her off quickly when she brought up the issue of the ball throwing. "The trouble with you administrators," he said, "is that you quickly forget how things really are in a classroom. You've been taking graduate courses that fill you with all these dreamy ideas about pedagogy, but you forget that kids often act like kids and sometimes they need shock therapy to get them to pay attention so they will learn. I've been using this 'stress ball' for years and I like it. When kids stop paying attention, I throw it at them. It gets them back in the game. It works."

Pauline started to suggest that perhaps something less violent would work just as well, but Williams raised his hand dismissively and said, "This part of the conversation is over. I've been around a long time; I know what I'm doing."

"Well," Pauline responded, "I hope we can keep talking about this. I don't think throwing things at students is a good approach to learning."

"Talk all you want," Williams replied, "but I'm just going to keep doing what works."

After leaving, Pauline realized she now had to decide whether she would pursue this matter further and, if so, how. What do you suggest?

Discussion

The primary question here is whether Mr. Williams's use of the stress ball technique is ethical. Is it ever appropriate to throw anything at a student? If so, what are the boundaries on this sort of behavior? And what are the consequences, intended and unintended?

Defenders of Williams's approach would argue that student attentiveness is important to learning and, if tossing a soft ball at an inattentive student corrects that behavior, the end is accomplished and no harm is done. But critics would counter that the action itself contains a lesson: A violent act—however harmless in a physical sense—suggests to students that violence can be productive and helpful. The immediate effectiveness of the act, the critics would argue, is heavily outweighed by the broader impression it conveys.

A critic might also ask where the line is drawn. If some violence is acceptable, how much? Can an eraser be thrown? A pen? A harder ball? If a school tolerates any violence in the relationship between teachers and students, how can it effectively constrain the implementation of that behavior?

Embedded in this case as well is a serious dilemma for Pauline. She is new to this school and to her role as an administrator. Like all novices, she doesn't want to get off on the wrong foot by butting heads with a senior teacher. On the other hand, she has observed something she thinks is dead wrong. She wonders how she should proceed.

Since she doesn't know whether the stress ball technique has been observed by other adults in the school—or whether any other teachers employ this or similar techniques, her first step should be a conversation with the principal. Before having that conversation, she might also find it useful to discuss her concerns with someone outside the school, a former colleague or a professor from her graduate program, for example, to help determine if she's right to be concerned about this. Is she missing anything that might help her see some validity in the stress-ball approach?

If she remains convinced that some corrective action is necessary, she should try to work with the principal to accomplish that. Perhaps the solution will be the establishment of a school policy, worked out with the faculty, which prohibits any act of violence against a student for any purpose and offers some definitions of proscribed activities. Or perhaps the impropriety of such violence is already widely understood as at least an implicit school policy and the real problem is that Mr. Williams is violating a school norm. In that case, she and the principal will need to devise a strategy for ending his use of the stress ball.

If the principal doesn't agree that Mr. Williams is acting improperly, Pauline has a larger problem. She can persist in trying to make her case persuasively to the principal in an effort to change his mind. Failing that, she might be able to gain his acquiescence in bringing the matter to the whole faculty as a policy issue. She can also seek another conversation with Mr. Williams, hoping it will be more successful than the first.

Pauline may also find it helpful to recognize that some victories take time, that this is a change she will have to keep pursuing as her role within the school crystallizes. Only then, perhaps, will she have more opportunities to persuade her colleagues that the ethical culture of her school needs to rule out any violence against students as an absolute touchstone of teacher behavior.

WHO SPEAKS FOR THE STUDENT?

Here is another situation concerning a student, a special education teacher, and colleagues at the school. Bill has been a consulting teacher in special education at the middle school for five years. He supervises educational technicians and together they support the students who compose Bill's caseload for one of the teams in the school.

Prior to an incident with Jimmy, Bill had often worried about the assistant principal's discipline strategy. He appeared to be meting out harsher punishments to certain students who lacked a parental advocate and were thus less likely to resist or challenge him. Bill also worried that the assistant principal's actions too often responded to teachers' desires to remove students who were behavioral challenges and too rarely considered the best interests of the students. In two particular instances where students were removed from classes for an entire year, Bill found that their removal had not improved the learning environment in those classes.

In one of those cases, a student who was the center of all the classroom disruptions was not disciplined or removed because her parents were well educated and advocated for their child when the assistant principal attempted to have their child permanently removed from class. The student who was removed was a less frequent problem, but neither of her parents came to her defense. The operative policy thus seemed to be that the assistant principal would remove problem students from classes only when minimal or no resistance from parents was anticipated.

One of the students on Bill's caseload was Jimmy, a seventh grader who was having a difficult adolescence. His mother was a substance abuser who was largely absent from Jimmy's life. Jimmy lived with his aunt, who cared about her nephew's welfare but who worked long hours at a local factory and had limited time to participate in any of Jimmy's school activities. When Bill was notified that Jimmy was kicked out of science class, he went to speak with the science teacher after school.

When he asked her about her decision to have this student removed, Bill tried to keep an open mind. He listened to the teacher and let her know that he understood her frustration. He chose not to argue with her. Instead he asked probing questions to get at the root of the problem she was having with Jimmy. She explained that Jimmy was not working with his partner in lab. He sat next to her, but he did not participate in lab work. She also noted that he sometimes fell asleep in her class. She mentioned that she could not help this student and removing him from her class would send a message to him that he "needed to get his act together."

As they talked further, the science teacher noted a graver concern. She said that she had heard that Jimmy was suspected in some of the recent thefts in the school and, though nothing had yet been missing from her supplies, she said that she was worried every time Jimmy walked into the storage room. As Bill thought about this later, he recalled a conversation with the principal about the disappearance of

(Continued)

(Continued)

some video equipment in which Jimmy's name was mentioned as a possible suspect. But there was no evidence linking Jimmy to the theft and no action had been taken against him.

Bill assumed that he and the assistant principal were the only parties to that discussion, but now he had doubts. He noted that he had often seen the science teacher sitting in the assistant principal's office in the morning. They might well have been having social conversations, but Bill had to wonder if the assistant principal had violated Jimmy's right to confidentiality and the presumption of innocence. Had he shared with the science teacher information about Jimmy, perhaps even false information, that should not have been shared with her that may have colored her judgment and increased her anxiety about him?

The next day, the assistant principal, the science teacher, Jimmy, his aunt, and Bill had a meeting to discuss Jimmy's situation. They reviewed the only other time Jimmy was sent to the office from this class. He had fallen asleep. Bill brought up Jimmy's grade from the previous quarter and noted that he received a 77, a passing grade, and that there were only three weeks until the end of school year. Bill recommended that Jimmy should be permitted to stay in the class so he could pass science for the year, that is, as long as he was willing to adjust his attitude. The assistant principal did not respond, yielding instead to the science teacher. She was adamant that Jimmy be removed from her class.

Bill was uncertain about how to proceed. He had worked with the science teacher for several years and generally liked and respected her as an educator. She was always willing to go the extra distance for her students and usually had their best interests at heart. So Bill was a little surprised by her reaction in this situation. She indicated that she had no tolerance for students who were unwilling to do their fair share of the work and who bring other students' performance down. But it also appeared to him that she was reacting to more than just Jimmy's behavior in her class, behavior which would not lead to removal in all cases, especially, Bill believed, in the case of students who had actively engaged parents. Was it that she had heard that Jimmy was suspected of being a thief that escalated her anxiety?

Bill later felt he should have argued more forcefully about the impact this decision would have on Jimmy and he should have expressed his feeling that the decision was not fair or equitable. But he was constrained because he had other students on his caseload in the science class, and he needed to maintain a good working relationship with this teacher. He wondered if he should go to the assistant principal and articulate his concerns about confidentiality and how this decision would impact Jimmy. He feared it would appear that he was attacking the assistant principal's authority or even questioning his integrity. He worried that such a conversation with the assistant principal would erode their professional relationship.

Bill decided instead to discuss his concerns with the special education director, indicating especially that the assistant principal appeared to be targeting students who had little or no family support. He did not mention the apparent breach of confidence. The director listened sympathetically but offered little mitigation of Bill's concerns. It is the science teacher's classroom, she told Bill, and unless the principal or assistant principal disagreed with the teacher's actions, Jimmy would be removed. Bill needed to support Jimmy, she pointed out, but not by challenging the orderly processes of the school.

Bill was left to wonder if he had fully met his ethical and professional obligations in this case.

Discussion

Here we need to examine the actions of all three of the professionals directly involved in this case: the special education consulting teacher, the science teacher, and the assistant principal. The assistant principal felt Jimmy was a problem to the school; the science teacher thought Jimmy was a problem to his classmates and thus to her. Bill thought the others were not giving adequate consideration to Jimmy's interests and were treating him differently from other students because he lacked articulate and protective parents; however, he worried that if he fought too forcefully there would be consequences in the future for other students on his caseload.

The assistant principal's primary obligations are to maintain order and discipline in the school and to support teachers in their efforts to maintain an effective learning environment in their classrooms. But he also shares with all other professionals in the school an obligation to act in the best interest of individual students and to balance their needs with those of the school community (Blase & Anderson, 1995; Sizer & Sizer, 1999). He also has an ethical obligation to maintain the confidentiality of students and to share information only with those who have a need to know.

We cannot be certain from the facts presented here if the assistant principal has acted unethically in sharing allegations about Jimmy stealing from the school with the science teacher. If he did so, he acted improperly. Since Jimmy has stolen nothing from her classroom, nor is there any evidence that he had stolen from anyone, there is no apparent need for her to know about the other suspicions. Such information could, and apparently did, diminish her regard for Jimmy and contribute to her decision to have him removed from her class.

Bill's broader concern that the assistant principal enforces discipline inequitably by acting more harshly in cases where he anticipates little parental resistance is significant. As a primary advocate for the interests of at-risk students, Bill cannot let this concern go unexpressed. At a minimum, he should gather available evidence to try to determine whether there is a demonstrable and consistent pattern of such inequity in the assistant principal's actions. If the evidence clearly supports Bill's suspicions, he has an obligation to present it to others.

A reasonable approach would be for Bill to consult with his supervisor and perhaps with other special education teachers who have similar caseloads in the school. This should help him confirm his suspicions or perhaps discover that others do not share his observations. If those concerns are shared by others, the next step would be for the special education director to meet with the assistant principal to discuss this concern about inequitable treatment and perhaps as well to reiterate the importance of maintaining confidentiality about individual students. If the assistant principal is defensive or resistant to these expressions from the special education department and indicates no plan or intention to alter his behavior, it would then be appropriate to take the concerns to the principal.

The science teacher may have acted improperly here by allowing her decision to seek Jimmy's removal from her class to be affected by information to which she should not have been privy. She is right to be concerned about the learning environment in her classroom, and she certainly has the right to seek help with a student whose behavior seems incorrigible and harmful to the collective learning process. But she is also obligated to base those judgments solely on her own balanced observations and to be certain that she is consistent and fair in her treatment of all students. If her actions with regard to Jimmy were colored by information about his behavior outside her class or if she acted differently than she would have with a disruptive student whose parents were more active advocates, then she has not met her fundamental obligations.

Bill has a significant dilemma in his case, but also a significant ethical obligation. One of the most common deterrents to ethical action is the fear of speaking up, the fear that doing the right thing will have costly consequences for the person who speaks up or for his constituents or clients (Chaleff, 2003; Plante, 2004). Silence, unfortunately, is often the safer course. But often it is the wrong one.

If Bill truly believes that the students for whom he is responsible are being treated unfairly and in ways that harm their best interests, he has an obligation to protect them. Recognizing that there is some risk in speaking up, he should be diligent in gathering evidence of the systematic inequities he alleges (Marshall & Oliva, 2006). But once he is certain that a pattern of unfairness exists, seeking to end it is the right thing for him to do.

These educators failed to make Jimmy's learning and well-being the foundation of their actions, and they failed to provide Jimmy with the right to learn and the guarantee of equal education. Jimmy was not treated fairly and equitably nor with dignity and respect, nor was he provided with the personal and academic support often required by at-risk students. It is important for educators and administrators to promote the success of all students by acting with integrity, fairness, and thoughtful consideration of individual needs. And we have to wonder what kind of climate exists in a school where a teacher has to worry that, if he advocates for a student, he is jeopardizing his relationship with administrators and colleagues.

These cases point to the central ethical dilemma in the relationship between teachers and students, the conflict between the needs of the collectivity and the needs of the individual. Schools are communities. They can succeed only when they operate in an orderly way according to policies that balance collective and individual interests (Sizer & Sizer, 1999). But such policies can never be perfect, nor perfectly adaptable, to every interaction between teachers and students. Hence the constant need to step back from the details of any particular situation and reflect on its broader meaning. What are the community interests? What are the individual student's interests? What is the nature of the conflict between them? How can a solution keep them in proper balance?

Teachers play a critical role in this, in balancing the individual and collective purposes of a school. They must have the courage to stand up for students when their interests are in jeopardy. But they must also recognize that the collective interests of the school community place some boundaries on the character of their advocacy (Enomoto & Kramer, 2007; Pellicer, 2003). Collegiality need not be the enemy of individual advocacy. In fact, in a healthy school environment, colleagues ought to welcome all efforts to serve the individual needs of students, even those that challenge teachers and administrators to adjust or change their practices. Openness to criticism and reflection are signs of good health in any organization (Barth, 2001; Berlak & Berlak, 1981; Pellicer, 2003). In schools, that is especially the case when the aim of such reflection is to support students and their learning.

As members of a faculty, teachers have a role in voicing concerns, bringing issues to the fore, and standing up for students' learning needs. At the same time, as members of communities with standing rules and policies, teachers have an obligation to respect the interests and motives of their colleagues, to follow established procedures, and recognize that the greatest good for the greatest number cannot always yield happy outcomes for everyone. Consensus and the adherence to precedent have an important role in a school community but so do openness and inquiry (Bryk & Schneider, 2002; Pellicer, 2003). Teachers have to be willing and able to participate fully in policymaking deliberations and help their fellow teachers continue to ponder and consider the impact of what they have decided and instituted (Marshall & Oliva, 2006; Meier, 2002).

Students have collective and individual interests; both must be served. Acting ethically can mean supporting existing policies as often as it means challenging them. But support or challenge should derive from the same source: careful contemplation of everyone's best interest, intelligent consultation, and proper consideration of the principles of ethical behavior.

Every case in this book, although focused on the relationships teachers have with other people in schools, ultimately returns to, and often hinges on, the central function of the school, that of the connection between teachers and students. So even though we will tease out issues that affect many relationships in the school community, we need to remember how much decision making in schools and by teachers must revolve around what is best for students and their learning.

For Reflection and Conversation

As you read the following vignettes of school situations from teachers' journals, consider first if they involve ethical issues. If so, how would you characterize the issues? How would you help the teacher sort out the issues? What ethical principles or decision rules might be helpful in examining the conflicts these situations present?

❖ ❖ ❖

1. A few weeks ago, my parents gave me a new puppy. I love the dog, but since I live alone in an apartment building, it didn't feel right to leave the puppy at home all day. I started to bring him to school, which delighted my first-grade students who quickly adopted him as their pet. The problem is that a new puppy demands a lot of

my attention during the day and sometimes distracts me from the lessons I am teaching and pulls me away from discussions with individual students. Bringing the puppy to school solves a personal problem for me, but is it right to do so in this way? Should the students' enjoyment of the puppy be a factor in this? My school has no policy on teachers bringing pets to school or even about teachers bringing their own children. Should it?

2. A student of mine has missed the last two weeks of school because she is back in the hospital for emotional reasons. After speaking to the guidance counselor, I decided not to give her make-up work. I chose instead to give her the grade she had earned just before she left. This was acceptable to guidance. Is it in her best interest not to overload her with work? Does this obligate me, out of fairness, to treat any student who misses significant work because of illness in the same way? Should I worry that this was too convenient a way to handle this because it relieved me of the burden of coming up with work for her to complete?

3. A student in my class told me that she had a friend who was cutting herself and had indicated she wanted to be dead. The friend was a student in our school, but I was not her teacher and did not know her personally. I did, however, know her mother who works out at my gym. I decided to call the mother rather than go through school channels, which might have given the girl a label or reputation she didn't deserve. The mother asked me to relay the complete conversation I had with the student in my class, her daughter's friend.

The problem was that my student had indicated that many of her friend's problems were related to difficulties with her mother, and I didn't want to share information with the mother that would be very hurtful to her. So I lied and told her that I didn't really know any details, only that her daughter was in trouble and I wanted to be sure she knew this. Should I have told the mother the full story as I heard it? Should I have called the mother at all? Should I have passed the original information on to the guidance department and made no contact with the mother? Should I have done nothing? What would the student who shared this information about her friend think if I did nothing?

4. The principal came to me to discuss two students' grades posted by a teacher who is a member of my department. I am not the department chair, but I have been a friend of the principal since we started our teaching careers together in this school more than a decade ago. The students' quarter grades did not average out over the year to a passing mark (70), but the teacher overrode the numerical average to allow the students to pass. The principal was not happy as she felt that, should anyone "do the math," he or she would see that the four quarters could not possibly average a 70 and that perhaps there had been a mistake or a misjudgment on the part of the teacher. Should I get involved in this? Should a teacher override a failing average at the end of the year if he feels that the student knows the subject matter even though the student did not do the everyday work? Can the principal ask a teacher to change a passing grade? Who is ultimately in charge of grades? Is it my job to talk to my colleague about this as a member of my department, or is assigning grades to students a professional prerogative?

5. I am a special education teacher in a high school. When one of the students I work with did not show up at school on the morning when he was scheduled to take a final exam, I went to his house, got him out of bed, and drove him to school. Should I have gone to his house or allowed him to pay the price for getting a zero on his final? Knowing that if I did not show up at his house he would not have gone to school, I still wonder how much is too much? Is it fair to do this for one student if I haven't done it for others in similar circumstances?

4

Important Pieces
of the Puzzle

Teachers and Parents

Parents are essential partners in the learning process. But parents vary widely in the way they approach this partnership. Some have great respect for teachers and schools and are anxious to work closely and supportively with those to whom they entrust their child's education. Others see the school as a necessary evil, or at least a junior partner, in their child's learning. They want the best for their children but are not convinced that individual teachers or the school community can provide what they want. Other parents are simply disengaged. They send their children to school and assume that is sufficient to fulfill their responsibilities for their children's education. They pay little attention to what happens at school or to their children's intellectual or social development. Not uncommonly, parents are much more concerned about what is best for their own children and much less concerned about the learning or welfare of other children (Bryk & Schneider, 2002).

Teachers must juggle parents of all these types, seeking effective partnerships with each of them but on widely varying terms. Inevitably some of these relationships yield tensions, disagreements, and even hostility. Frequently, as well, teachers find themselves in situations that raise complex ethical questions about when to consult parents, what to tell them, and how and when to respond to parental requests for certain kinds of action (Blase & Anderson, 1995; Sockett, 1990).

In the following cases, we explore several common interactions between teachers and parents, each of them posing a set of ethical uncertainties for the teachers involved. One of the things we will see in these cases is how important it is for teachers to recognize the character of the ethical dilemmas they are facing. Too often, unfortunately, the easy response—the one that will please the parents—may not be the one that serves the best interests of the student or the school. Hence the teacher's obligation to professional standards and to the best interests of the school community may be in conflict with parental desires. This is rarely a comfortable situation for a teacher.

WHAT HAPPENS IN THE LIBRARY STAYS IN THE LIBRARY

Jane is a school librarian who is highly regarded for her ability to adjust to changing circumstances. That ability was sorely tested after budget cuts eliminated 25 hours of paraprofessional help Jane had been getting. To keep her program intact, she turned to parent volunteers. She thought the time and effort invested in training, scheduling, and supervising more than 40 parents was worth it if it meant that she could maintain services for the 400 students and 50 staff members in her elementary school.

The volunteers were eager and reliable, and they responded quickly to Jane's training sessions. One of the issues on which she focused was the importance of confidentiality, specifically avoiding gossip about students. To drive the point home in her orientation sessions, she asked parents the rhetorical question, "How would you feel if a parent discussed your child's behavior in the library with other parents?" She also required that all volunteers sign a confidentiality pledge.

But as the year went on, some volunteers left and others joined. Jane had little time to orient the new volunteers and she neglected to ask many of them to sign the confidentiality pledge. She came to regret that in January when a difficult situation unfolded.

Jane's principal, Cynthia, came to her office one morning to report a phone call she received the night before from an angry parent. The parent had been at a local fast food restaurant and had overheard a woman in the next booth describing to a friend the misbehavior in the school library of the angry parent's daughter. "She dresses like a slut," she heard the woman say, "and she swears like a trooper. And she never reads anything, just holds her cell phone under the table and texts her friends." The parent decided not to confront the woman, whom she did not know, but to complain to the principal. Complain she did in a long, angry telephone conversation. She demanded that the gossiping volunteer be "fired." Cynthia responded that she would look into this and report back. The parent's description of the subject of her complaint made it clear to Cynthia that the volunteer in question was a woman named Cheryl.

Jane was deeply distressed when Cynthia told her about this and agreed that such gossip and violations of confidentiality were unacceptable. Cynthia asked Jane to confront Cheryl, to explain what she'd done wrong, and to "put her on a short leash." Jane agreed to do so.

But when Cheryl appeared for her volunteer assignment the next day, Jane could not bring herself to confront Cheryl directly. Instead she sent a memo to all the volunteers reminding them of the importance of confidentiality and requiring those who had never signed the confidentiality pledge to do so. Later in the week, when Jane ran into Cynthia after a faculty meeting, Cynthia asked her how the confrontation with Cheryl had gone and whether she could report back to the angry parent that the problem had been addressed and would not recur. Jane said that "everything has been taken care of and it won't happen again."

Discussion

Two goals ought to guide Jane's actions here. One is to prevent a recurrence of the gossiping about a student of which Cheryl was apparently guilty. The second is to maintain the vitality of the volunteer program. Both serve the broader purposes of the school.

Jane took the path of least resistance in dealing with the problem caused by Cheryl. Instead of confronting Cheryl directly, she treated the problem more generically with a communication to all the volunteers. That may have been the right course if she was concerned that a confrontation, while perhaps chastening to Cheryl, would have undermined her relationship with other volunteers and thus threatened the volunteer program. Obviously, dealing with colleagues or employees is not the same as dealing with volunteers. Jane decided that she could accomplish her two primary objectives with the least conflict by avoiding a direct confrontation with Cheryl.

Cheryl's actions are serious, however, and Jane would need to be convinced that she could stop Cheryl and other volunteers from gossiping with her indirect approach. If she had doubts about that, then it was her obligation to have a one-on-one conversation with Cheryl. This need not be a "confrontation," and it might be possible to avoid a direct reference to the specific complaint. Nevertheless, it is important that Cheryl understand the value of confidentiality.

It is always difficult to criticize directly the behavior or actions of another person with whom we work. But sometimes there is no other way to serve the broader interests of a school. Hurt feelings, despite our best efforts at diplomacy, may occur.

There is another issue here. When Jane reported to Cynthia that "everything has been taken care of," she may have been misleading her principal. Cynthia had asked her to confront Cheryl directly. Jane did not do that. Jane may well believe that the approach she followed was the best in this situation, and if so, she should have explained her approach and her rationale to Cynthia. Allowing Cynthia to believe that a direct conversation had occurred, when none had, was deceit. Deceit is rarely an ethical solution, and it certainly would not be here.

A QUICK DECISION

After a decade as a public school tennis coach, Mark had just taken a new job at a private high school. When he met with his athletic director, Skip, the name of one of the new players came up. Julie Smith, a tenth grader, was an especially talented player. Skip told him to be wary, though, of Julie's mother, Janice. The Smiths lived more than 30 miles away but sent their daughter to the school because Janice Smith had gone to the school herself and was an influential alumna.

A few days after the meeting with the athletic director, Mark received a call from Julie's mother. She was friendly and welcoming. She told Mark how happy she was to have a new tennis coach because she had been unhappy with the former one. This year, Mrs. Smith expected Julie to win the state's high school singles' tournament. She came across as a charming and convincing person.

During the discussion, Janice Smith informed him that her daughter would not practice with the team during the season. Instead, she said, Julie would practice with her own coach at the tennis club near her home. She apologized for this but explained that because they lived so far away it was impossible for her to come every day to pick up her daughter at the end of practice and Julie was too young to drive herself. This way Julie could take the school's bus home at the end of classes and practice nearby. Without really thinking about it, Mark agreed, and the conversation ended pleasantly. After Mark hung up the telephone, however, he remembered Skip's caution and wondered why he had agreed so quickly to this plan.

A few days later, all potential players attended a mandatory team meeting to discuss the upcoming season and Mark's policies for the team. One of those was that all practices were mandatory. At the end of the meeting, the three seniors on the team asked to speak to him. One said, "Coach, we'd like to talk to you about something before things turn out like they did last year." The girls described the tension on the team because Julie had not practiced with them last year. The girls said they thought it was unfair and led to disunity on the team. One girl commented, "I realize that Julie's parents have to drive 30 miles to pick her up, but my parents drive 25 miles to get me, so why shouldn't I be able to miss practices too?" They also thought it was wrong for Julie to have the benefit of a personal coach because her parents were rich when most of their parents could not or would not pay for personal coaching. Mark thanked them for talking to him and told them he would consider everything they said.

As Mark thought about his acquiescence to Mrs. Smith's request regarding her daughter's tennis practice schedule, he began to ask himself several questions. Was his decision fair to the other players on the tennis team? If he were a member of this team, how would he feel if a coach made a decision such as this? Is the decision in the best interest of the entire team? Will this decision make the team "better" or "worse" in the long run? Does he have the right to renege on the agreement he made with Julie's mother?

Breaking the agreement with Mrs. Smith could lead to a contentious battle with an influential school parent. Mrs. Smith might decide to withdraw her daughter from the tennis team altogether, causing the team to lose its most skilled player. But some possible outcomes of maintaining the agreement with Mrs. Smith could be a loss of respect for him from the tennis players and their parents, a sense of disappointment from the athletic director for allowing this unfair treatment to occur, and an overall decrease in morale among the team members.

What should Mark do?

Discussion

The first question Mark should ask himself is this: What is the purpose of team sports in a school setting? Presumably, he would respond that it is to inculcate certain values like hard work, shared purpose, physical exercise, and mutual interdependence. Then he would need to ask whether tennis is different from other sports either in its purposes or in the way those purposes might be accomplished.

If Mark concluded that tennis was unique and that the school's purposes in supporting a tennis program could be achieved without all the players practicing together, he should explain that to all the players on the team. If he comes to that conclusion, however, he would be obligated to permit any or all of the players to practice with personal coaches. Having different policies for different players would be difficult to justify under any circumstances.

If, however, Mark concludes that tennis is not unique, that team unity depends in large part on the team practicing together, then he has to reassess his acquiescence to Janice's request that Julie practice on her own. He would be obligated then to explain to Julie and to Janice that he had thought further about the request and realized that his initial response was in error. If Julie is a member of the team, she has to practice with the team. While this might cause Julie to leave the team, and thus deprive the team of its best player, that is a risk that Mark has to take.

It is often the case that coaches and others in the school confront powerful conflicts when an excellent athlete violates the rules, underperforms in class, or seeks special accommodations. Should the star athlete be treated differently from other students for the benefit of the team? In general, the answer to that question has to be no. On a professional team or other team not in a school setting, the answer might be different. Those coaches or team owners may be willing to treat some players differently because of their special talents. But in a school, it is important to maintain the primacy of the school's broader, collective objectives (Bryk & Schneider, 2002; Meier, 2002; Pellicer, 2003). Everyone likes winning teams, but everyone should be cautious about making compromises to secure them.

Mark's primary goal here is not to keep Julie happy and on the team nor is it necessarily to keep the other players happy. It is to run a tennis program in a school that serves the educational and developmental purposes of its students. It is also to run a program that treats all participants fairly and equally to the maximum extent possible.

There is another ethical consideration here. Mark has made a commitment to Janice. He did so without careful consideration, but surely Janice will feel that Mark is obligated to keep that commitment. Is it ethical for Mark to tell her that he has changed his mind and that Julie must practice with the team? The answer is yes. Commitments are important, and keeping them is generally the right thing to do. But sometimes commitments are made in haste and subsequent reconsideration casts them in a different light. Furthermore, new information can arise that causes us to reconsider the propriety of commitments we have entered.

That is the case here. Had Mark reconsidered his commitment to Janice, especially after hearing from other members of the team, it was reasonable for him to contact Janice and explain why he had changed his mind. It can never be ethical to keep a commitment that violates an ethical principle. If you agreed to meet your friend in front of the First National Bank at 2 p.m. to give him a ride to the airport and then discovered when you arrived that your friend had robbed the bank and wanted you to be the getaway driver, the right action would be not to keep your commitment to take him to the airport. Once Mark decided that the purposes of the school were best served by having all the players on the tennis team practice together, keeping a commitment to Janice to do otherwise could not be justified on ethical grounds.

BOWLING ALONG

Brad is a high school biology teacher. This year, one of the juniors in his class is Tom, a student who wants to go to college but pays too little attention in class and is inconsistent in completing his assignments. Nevertheless, Brad sees a lot of potential in Tom and has decided to "light a fire under him." He has asked Tom to be his lab assistant on a project Brad has undertaken as part of his work toward a graduate degree at the state university. He hopes that this special attention will encourage Tom's interest in biology and lead to improved performance in class and perhaps in his other courses as well.

Brad is also an avid bowler. Tom's father owns the town's largest bowling alley where Brad bowls at least twice a week. One night recently, when Brad was paying his bill, Tom's father said that it was "on the house." He said Brad could bowl for free whenever he wished. Although Brad was initially pleased with this since his weekly bowling costs often exceeded $50, he knew that it had to be because of his interest in Tom. Brad knew his school had a pretty rigid policy prohibiting gifts from parents, and he did not want to violate that. He thanked Tom's father and said he thought he should pay for his own bowling. Tom's father laughed off the objection by telling him all teachers could bowl there for free, so Brad shouldn't be concerned about it. Brad left without paying for his bowling, pleased with the savings he could now anticipate.

Was this the appropriate response from Brad?

Discussion

One of the keys to acting ethically in any situation is to recognize and acknowledge when you confront an ethical issue. It is also helpful to try to categorize that issue because useful rules and principles often apply in specific kinds of ethical situations (Enomoto & Kramer, 2007). The issue here involves gifts.

Gift rules are vexing in every institution, and they are especially troublesome in schools. Gift giving complicates the relationship between parents and teachers. Parents value the hard work that teachers have done to improve the learning of their children, so often their only purpose in making the gift is gratitude. But it is hard to separate gifts of that sort from gifts that are intended to foster a special relationship between teacher and student or to bribe a teacher to give more attention or higher grades to a student. Given the difficulty in assessing the motives of the gift giver, most schools have policies that limit or prohibit gift giving by parents or students.

The challenge for Brad in this case is to understand that Tom's father is offering him a gift. It may not be something he can hold in his hand, but it is something of value, the normal definition of a gift. There are several ways in which Brad could convince himself that the school's gift rules ought not to apply, that he can accept free bowling. He could persuade himself, for example, that the bowling occurs outside of school and is unrelated to his teaching responsibilities. Or he could believe that the offer of free bowling to all teachers cancels out any special value for him, so it obviates the need to treat this as a gift situation. Or, of course, he could tell himself that since Tom's father spends nothing and loses nothing by allowing Brad to bowl for free this is not really something of value; therefore, it is not a gift.

But if Brad were to apply the rule of publicity here he would have a hard time convincing himself or anyone else that free bowling is not a gift. And, unless there had been a long-standing practice of allowing all teachers to bowl for free and other teachers had taken advantage of that, it would be difficult for Brad to convince himself or anyone else that this gift was not the result of having Tom as his student. And it matters little where the gift exchange actually occurs if the gift is the result of a relationship between a teacher and student. So all of the dodges Brad might use to convince himself of the propriety of accepting the offer of free bowling really do not stand up to scrutiny. It is unlikely that Brad could convince any reasonable person this was not a gift that resulted from his role as teacher of the gift giver's son.

Then the question is: Can Brad legitimately accept this gift? And the answer to that depends on the school's gift rules. Brad would be wise in this case to review those rules and, if they are unclear about the propriety of accepting free bowling, then to consult with his principal or others in the school and seek their advice. If the principal, for example, indicates that Brad violates no rule or the spirit of any rule by accepting free bowling, it would be wise for Brad to get that determination in writing in case questions are subsequently raised about the ethics of accepting this benefit.

If Brad determines that the free bowling is a gift and it is not appropriate for a teacher to accept such a gift, then he should return to the bowling alley, explain the school's policies to Tom's father, and compensate him for the bowling for which he was not charged.

There is an important lesson in this case for all teachers: Beware parents bearing gifts. Many of those are well intended and have no strings attached. But that matters little. The task for teachers is not to try to sort out the motives of the gift givers. It is to protect the integrity of the school by ensuring that no student, no parent, and no member of the community comes to believe that the interaction between a teacher and a student was affected by a form of bribery called a gift.

WALKING AWAY

As the director of the middle school play, it was Phil's responsibility to remain with his actors and crew at the conclusion of rehearsal until they left to walk home or their parents picked them up. This was the part of extracurricular activities that Phil liked the least because there were always some parents who came late, and Phil often had to wait around for an hour or more after rehearsal before he could go home.

Aaron was often the last to leave. Normally his father picked him up, and he seemed to be a person who was perpetually late, always apologetic, always with a new excuse for his tardiness. One warm afternoon, Phil decided to wait with Aaron outdoors to enjoy the nice weather. As usual, Aaron's father was the last to arrive.

When he did appear, nearly 30 minutes after the end of the rehearsal, Phil noticed several things that bothered him. When the father drove into the schoolyard, he parked the car rather crookedly in a spot reserved for handicapped drivers. When he got out of the car and walked towards them, he seemed unsteady on his feet. And when they engaged in the normal small talk about why he was late, he seemed to slur his words a little, and Phil thought he detected the smell of alcohol. Phil asked him, "Are you sure you're okay to drive?"

Aaron's father gave him a withering look and responded angrily, "What are you accusing me of?" Phil said apologetically, "I'm not accusing you of anything, I was just wondering if maybe it wouldn't be better if I drove you home or called a cab."

The father responded abruptly, "Please mind your own business." Then he turned to Aaron and said, "Let's go." Aaron gave Phil a forlorn look and then slowly turned and headed toward the car. When both were in the car, the father backed quickly out of the parking space and sped off.

Should Phil have acted differently in this case?

Discussion

Teachers concerned about the welfare of their students often confront a painful dilemma in deciding when they can or should intervene in family matters. If a parent appears to be a danger to a student, when is it a teacher's responsibility to take action to protect the student? And does that responsibility extend beyond the school grounds and the school day? In general, we might respond that the teacher's responsibility is for the student's learning and that all other matters of the student's development are a parental responsibility.

But it is rarely that simple. "Learning" can be very broadly defined, and good teachers often recognize that learning is contextual and occurs most effectively when students are healthy, safe, and happy. The home lives of students may not be the responsibility of teachers, but they often intersect with the work that teachers do at school (Marshall & Oliva, 2006).

In this case, Phil is genuinely torn. He recognizes that there are limits on how and when he should intervene in family matters, and he does not wish to violate those limits. But he also recognizes that his student, Aaron, may be at serious risk in this case. If the father is indeed drunk, as Phil suspects, allowing Aaron to ride in a car with him is dangerous.

Phil does have an ethical obligation to look out for Aaron's welfare. If he chooses to act on that obligation, however, he is uncertain about what he should do. Should he confront Aaron's father, accuse him of being inebriated, and plead with him not to drive with his son? Should he express his concerns to Aaron and ask Aaron not to get in the car? Should he call the police or some school official to report the father? Or should he assume that he has fulfilled his obligation and done everything possible in this case when he asked Aaron's father whether he was okay to drive?

There is no easy or comforting answer here, but two important considerations should help Phil shape his response. One is that this interaction is occurring on school grounds, and Phil and Aaron are there because they have been engaged in an extracurricular activity. If, in this place and at this time, a stranger were trying to lure Aaron into his car, there could be little doubt about Phil's obligation to care for Aaron. The question then is whether that obligation diminishes when the threat to a student comes from a parent not a stranger.

It would seem that the obligation remains substantial and that simply asking the father if he's okay to drive does not fully satisfy it. It would not be inappropriate for Phil to indicate to the father that he believes he has had too much to drink to drive safely and that he should not be taking his son in the car under those conditions. It might also be prudent for Phil to speak directly to Aaron, to explain the danger he perceives, and to ask Aaron not to get into the car. If neither of those approaches succeeds and Aaron and his father drive off, Phil should then feel no hesitation about informing school officials or the police. Drunk driving is a crime. In this case, it is a crime that endangers the welfare of a student. Perhaps Phil could not succeed in preventing Aaron and his father from driving off, but he is obligated to do everything he can to accomplish that and then, if that fails, to report the crime to proper authorities.

These cases describe some of the common dilemmas that teachers confront in their relations with parents. Parent-teacher relationships are usually healthy, and parents often serve as important partners in the work of a school. But the highest priority for most parents is the learning and welfare of their own children, and when that conflicts— or is perceived to conflict—with the broader purposes of the school, parents will usually take the side of their children.

This puts teachers and school administrators in a difficult position because, while they too care about the welfare and learning of individual children, the collective needs and values of the school are often more apparent to them than to parents. So they find themselves juggling or balancing parents' demands with the often conflicting policies and objectives of the school they serve (Blase & Anderson, 1995).

Teachers may find themselves defending or protecting the interests of the school from the desires of parents to secure some treatment for their children that is at odds with those broader interests. In those instances, as the cases here suggest, it is important for teachers to recognize their primary obligations and to explain those clearly and directly to parents. Sometimes that may yield unhappy parents, but making every parent happy can never be the true test of a school's success. We must adhere to Dewey's (1915) ideal, "What the best and wisest parent wants for his own child, that must the community want for all of its children," and help parents to be good and wise.

For Reflection and Conversation

As you read the following vignettes of school situations from teachers' journals, consider first if they involve an ethical issue. If so, how would you characterize the issue? What ethical principles or decision rules might be helpful in sorting through the conflicts these situations present?

❖ ❖ ❖

1. *An elementary teacher writes:* I coach my daughter's little league team. I am amazed at how some people act at events like this. We are working with young people who are learning the sport, yet some parents are critical of coaches and of their own kids. Good behavior sometimes takes a backseat to being fanatical sports fans—even at little league. I see this as a definite right versus wrong situation, but others consider that these parents have a right to express themselves this way. Here's what I wonder: Should I speak to parents who I believe are acting improperly at these games? Is that part of my responsibility as a professional who works with young people? Would my obligations be different if this were happening at a game involving a school team?

2. *A high school teacher writes:* I had a recent visit from parents of a student of mine seeking his admission to our honors diploma program. I've been reluctant about this, but I wonder if I should share the reasons for my reluctance with the parents. Their son is a pretty typical high school boy, not particularly interested in the details of his work or his progress. The tests and papers he writes in school are generally quite mediocre and do not reflect much preparation or thought on his part. On the other hand, his homework is always accurate, neat, and prompt. This has led me to wonder if the parents are doing his homework for him or heavily coaching him, although I have no proof of that. With his homework scores added in, his grades are high enough for the honors diploma program, but I seriously doubt that he has earned it. What should I do?

3. *A fifth-grade teacher writes:* Today a female student came running into school after recess covered in white powder. The nurse investigated and learned that the powder came from a pile of leftover field-lining chalk, which the maintenance crew had placed near a dumpster. A group of students had been creating "chalk balls" and were throwing them at each other when a female onlooker was hit. The nurse called poison control and washed the student's eyes out. The girl appeared to be fine, but she said her eyes stung a little. Following protocol, the nurse contacted the parents while I talked to the other students.

I determined that this was simply a case of a group of friends who made some poor choices. No harm was intended. The principal and I met with the boy who threw the chalk. He was sincerely remorseful for his actions, explained that he did not mean to hit her, and asked if the girl was okay.

Later that evening, I received a very angry e-mail from the girl's parents wondering why the police had not been called, if the substance had been tested for anthrax, and if the student who threw the powder had been expelled. They demanded to know the name of the boy who had thrown the chalk since their daughter refused to name him. They intended to bring charges against him. The parents copied the e-mail to the superintendent and several members of the school board. How should I respond to the parents?

4. *A multiage primary teacher writes:* I had a first grader with untreated attention deficit disorder. It took a while to convince the parents that she needed to be diagnosed and treated with medication and special diet. The parents have no skills to deal with her. The school convinced the parents to have her medications given at school because they are too disorganized to be sure she gets them in the morning. And they often do not send the right food—or any food—with her to school. I have been keeping meals in my supply closet so she has food she can eat when she needs it.

Am I wrong to do this? Should I provide food to be sure there is some at school that the child could eat? Is it enabling the parents? What is more important—the welfare of the child or the parents learning how to take responsibility? If I take extra measures like this with one child, am I obligated to do so with others who have similar problems at home? Under what conditions should a teacher assume responsibilities for the health and welfare of a child if he or she believes that parents are not managing that responsibility properly?

5. *A high school English teacher writes:* At the awards assembly this year, I was shocked when Mary received the social studies prize for seniors. I had taught Mary in

two English classes during her years at our school and never found her to be particularly interested in her work nor serious about improvement. It was hard for me to believe that she could be so much better in social studies than she was in English. When I mentioned this to some other teachers the next day, they indicated that they, too, were surprised that Mary had qualified for any award.

On Saturday, I stopped by the Ford dealership to get some work done on my car and happened to notice that one of my colleagues, Mr. Larson, was working there as a salesman. On Monday at school, I mentioned this to one of the other teachers who said to me with a smirk, "Now you should get it. Mr. Larson has been working part-time selling cars for years and the dealership is owned by Mary's father. I think that may explain why she won the social studies prize!"

I was troubled by this information and wondered what, if anything, I should do about it.

PART III

Acting Ethically: Teachers and Colleagues

Acting morally is behaving as if everything we do matters.

—Gloria Steinem

5

Trust and Respect

Teachers as Colleagues

Workplace relationships are a challenge in any institutional setting. The collective effectiveness of any organization is dependent on the ability of employees to work well together, to harness their skills and energy to shared purposes. Nowhere is that more critical than in a school where the relationships among teachers and administrators play a large role in shaping outcomes (Donaldson, 2006). Nevertheless, teachers, like other people, often have to decide what is more important, adhering to values and best practice or maintaining cordial relationships with those with whom they work closely (Goleman, Boyatzis, & McKee, 2002).

The core elements of successful working relationships in a school are trust and respect (Meier, 2002; Nash, 1996; Tschannen-Moran, 2006). Where trust and respect are mutual and widespread, opportunities to accomplish shared objectives flourish. Trust and respect require that colleagues understand their professional obligations and work individually and collectively to meet them, that they are open and honest in their interactions with each other, and that their decision making puts the interests of their school and their students above their self-interests (Meier, 2002).

But individual interactions among faculty members can be fraught with ethical challenges. Teachers do not always define professional obligations in the same way. Administrators sometimes play— or are perceived to play—favorites (Blase & Blase, 2002). In their desire to help their students, teachers sometimes trespass the boundaries of the teacher's role. Some people in a school may know personal information about a colleague that concerns them, or they may see behavior that troubles them.

Most of us are taught from a young age to mind our own business. In schools, that notion is often linked to the autonomy so valued by teachers (Lortie, 1975). Teachers are permitted to run their own classrooms and employ teaching methods they think work best with their students. The unspoken *quid pro quo* is "You let me teach my way, I'll let you teach yours."

Minding one's own business may be a useful starting point in our interactions with others, but sometimes it is the wrong response to an ethical dilemma. Sometimes it is our ethical responsibility to examine, question, and even challenge the actions of our colleagues. Simply deferring to the questionable behavior of a colleague may conflict with the best interests of students and the school. It is often easier to do or say nothing, especially for those who are not in positions of administrative responsibility. But when we allow improper behavior to go unquestioned or unchallenged, we diminish the collective enterprise for which we are all responsible. Risking scorn in the teacher's lounge may be the only proper course when confronted with damaging information about a colleague.

The best safeguards for the integrity of school employees are clear and consensual policies, frequent conversation about those policies and their application, and an understanding that every employee is a guardian of those policies and the values they are designed to serve. When we detect unethical behavior in our colleagues and do not question or challenge it, we have neglected our own ethical obligations (Enomoto & Kramer, 2007; Plante, 2004).

The cases presented here offer several examples of behavior by one school employee that raises troubling questions for a colleague. In each, we will see the importance of recognizing when an ethical issue has emerged, carefully weighing individual obligations, consulting with others to determine the proper course of action, and—most important—acting (Chaleff, 2003).

WHAT TO DO ABOUT THE TEST?

Linda was in her second year as a full-time teacher in a relatively small middle school. Her first year had been very difficult. She had come to rely on the support of several of her older colleagues, especially Karen, a music teacher, to help her survive. She and Karen had become good friends. Linda's second year was going along much more smoothly than the first because her confidence in her teaching abilities and her contributions to the school were increasing. But in March, she found herself facing a dilemma for which none of her training had prepared her.

The state assessments mandated by the No Child Left Behind (NCLB) regulations meant the entire school was involved in test taking for a week. Most of Linda's students seemed to take them in stride, and she felt she had done a good job of preparing them for the test. A few of her students did not take the test with the rest of the class because of accommodations determined in Pupil Evaluation Team (PET) meetings. One of her students, Kyle, received such accommodations as a special education student. He was able to take the language arts portions of the test in an alternate setting. Karen, the music teacher, was available to assist students with accommodations because there were no music classes on testing days.

As she was packing up the completed tests, Linda decided to scan through them. She was stunned as she read Kyle's beautifully written essay. The boy who was in special education for writing and could barely scrawl out a sentence on any form of written assignment had somehow pieced together a top-level essay *in someone else's handwriting.* Kyle clearly did not write the piece.

Linda knew the school would be in big trouble if the teachers were found to be submitting work that did not belong to the students. But Linda's closest friend on the faculty had supervised Kyle's test and was likely to have been the one who wrote his essay. What would happen to her if Linda were to blow the whistle? Would she lose her job? Linda certainly needed to think this over before she took action of any sort, yet she knew she had to think quickly.

Her first impulse was to run to the special education offices to show them the essay and ask questions. It was not fair that Kyle would test better than her students who tried harder and had more ability. It was not fair to the other special education students who didn't receive this extra help. Or did they? What if the whole department engaged in similar activities?

Before acting further, Linda caught up with Kyle's special education instructor to ask some general questions about his testing situation. She learned that Kyle was the only student who was monitored by Karen during testing. A full-time special education teacher or an education technician who worked in that department monitored all the other students. Linda was reassured that the special education department had followed the testing protocol.

(Continued)

(Continued)

As Linda considered her options, she could not help thinking about her friend Karen whom she knew to be a caring and compassionate person. Karen had nothing to gain professionally by Kyle's performance on the test since he was neither in the music program nor a student of hers. If she had, in fact, written his essay, she could only have done it to help him—or perhaps even to help Linda. Or maybe Karen had not actually written the essay; she had just copied over what Kyle wrote because his handwriting was so bad. Perhaps it was his thinking and merely Karen's writing. But Linda doubted that since she knew how Kyle struggled to verbalize his thoughts.

Karen was just a few years older than Linda. She had two children, and she and her husband had just bought a house the previous summer. If Karen were to lose her job, it would be very hard for her to find another. Budget cutbacks across the state were causing music programs to be eliminated in many districts, and many experienced music teachers were unable to find jobs.

If Karen had written Kyle's essay, as Linda assumed, she had violated the state regulations about the exam which required that all work be done by the students whose names were on the tests. The principal was required to certify that every test met that standard. If Kyle's test was sent to the state in its current form and it was later determined to be invalid, all of the school's test results would be suspect. The community, the school board, and the parents would be in an uproar.

Linda wondered whether this was her problem and what, if anything, she should do about it.

Discussion

Few ethical situations are more complex or vexing than those that involve personal friends. Employment entails obligations but so does friendship. And when those conflict, it can be exceedingly difficult to plot an appropriate ethical course. So no one should underestimate the difficulty in which Linda finds herself in this case.

Linda's friendship with Karen has been very important to her in the difficult early days of her career. She feels a good deal of gratitude to Karen for that. But her obligation to Karen does not include, indeed should not include, a violation of Linda's own ethical standards. Even if Karen were her spouse or her child, Linda would be wrong to support the actions that Karen has taken here. The question, then, is not whether Linda should overlook what Karen has done and let it pass, but rather what action she must take to meet her ethical obligations.

Karen may not have intended harm. She may have believed that she was helping a troubled student complete a difficult task. But she clearly crossed a line. Helping a student and substituting the teacher's work for the student's are two very different things. By writing the student's essay and then submitting it as if it were his own, Karen has acted deceitfully. As a matter of pedagogy, there could be no way to defend this as a useful learning experience for Kyle. But, more important, Karen's actions are an affront to the values and ethical standards of the school in which she works. A simple application of the rule of universality—would it be acceptable if everyone did it?—highlights the inappropriateness of this action. So, too, the rule of publicity—could such an action be justified if it were publicized? No, again.

Linda has several choices. One is to go to Karen, explain to her what she has found, and ask Karen to admit her error to the principal before Kyle's essay is included in the packet to be sent to the state. Another option for Linda is to go directly to the principal, indicate what she has discovered, and allow the principal to take appropriate action. A third option is to do nothing, that is, to pretend that she never looked at the essays.

The third option is without ethical merit. By pursuing it, Linda would be participating in the deceit and would be as guilty of unethical action as Karen. The second option—taking her findings to the principal—would satisfy Linda's ethical obligation but incurs the risk of great potential harm to Karen. Karen's ability to take responsibility for her action and to minimize its impact is greatly diminished if she is not the one to report it and seek corrective action.

The first option, in which Linda speaks directly to Karen and urges her to describe what she has done to the principal, offers a reasonable balance between Linda's obligations to her school and to her friendship with Karen. If Karen acknowledges her action and seeks correction, this approach accomplishes the same purpose as direct communication with the principal, but it affords Karen an opportunity to minimize the damage to her own reputation and career.

Kidder (2003) offers some helpful guidance here. He describes three ethical paradigms, all of which are present in this case: truth versus loyalty, individual versus community, and short-term versus long-term results. Linda confronts the need to impose truth over loyalty, to place the standards and the needs of the school community over those of her personal relationship with Karen or even Karen's best interests, and to measure any course of action she chooses in terms of its long-term impact on her school community. It is important for individuals to do what is right, regardless of the outcome. But when there are alternative ways to do what is right, one may choose the course that is least damaging to the individuals involved.

Learning cannot occur where there is little to no confidence in the integrity of those who teach (Strike, 2007). One aspect of accountability as a teacher is professionalism—serving and defending the high standards of one's profession (Shapiro & Stepkovich, 2005). Karen was acting unprofessionally in this case; Linda was in a position to confront and correct her friend's lack of professionalism—and she was obligated to do so.

A PARENT'S WISHES

Peter, a guidance counselor, is struggling with a dilemma that is particularly troubling. The school year starts in another week and he has had several calls from parents of incoming sixth graders who are upset that their children have been assigned to Ms. Barter's language arts class. Each parent has said essentially the same thing. Ms. Barter has a reputation as a "mean" teacher who is especially tough on the children of upper-income parents. They worry that she will diminish the self-esteem of their children and perhaps give them lower grades than their ability merits for no reason other than some innate dislike of wealthy people.

Guidance counselors spend a lot of time carefully balancing classroom groups, abilities, behaviors, and course requests. They often have to defend student assignments, and the policy at this school is not to permit parents to dictate a child's assignment. So Peter has found himself playing a lot of defense lately, pointing out to the angry parents that Ms. Barter has been at the school for more than 20 years, that her evaluations have always been good, and that her classes perform well on standardized tests. When he asks callers if they can cite examples of Ms. Barter mistreating students in the way they have suggested, most have responded, "Well, that's her reputation," or "Everyone knows she hates rich kids."

Peter decides to have a conversation with Ms. Barter about this and catches up with her toward the end of the day when she has finished setting up the bulletin boards in her classroom. He has known her for a long time, and while she can be prickly at times, he feels comfortable being frank with her. He describes the tenor of the calls he has received without naming any names and asks whether she has a problem teaching the children of wealthier parents. She responds, "Not at all. In fact, I like it. Most of them need to be taken down a peg or two, and I feel I can make a valuable contribution to their learning by showing them they're no better than the other kids just because their parents have money. Sometimes, too, it's good for the whole class when I can make an example of one of the rich kids who screws up. Shows them they all get treated the same in my room."

"But don't you think that's unfair to kids who aren't responsible for how much money their parents have? Aren't you singling them out unfairly?"

"Well, that's my approach, Peter, and it's worked well for years. Some parents may complain about it at the beginning of the year, but by year's end, they're all happy their children were assigned to me because I get good test results."

Realizing there is not much to gain by going further with this conversation, Peter leaves. But he is uneasy. If it is Ms. Barter's teaching philosophy to mete out harsher treatment to some children because of the wealth of their parents, he does not think that satisfies the school's obligation to treat all students fairly and equitably. He decides to speak with the principal, Elizabeth, about this.

Elizabeth is starting her second year at the school and has begun to make a number of changes to improve the learning environment. She shares Peter's concern; in fact, she is very troubled by Ms. Barter's attitude and approach and decides to speak with her directly.

The next day when Elizabeth meets with Ms. Barter, she denies she ever said any of the things that Peter reported from their conversation. "I don't know where Peter got all that," she tells Elizabeth. "I never said anything of the sort. I treat all my students the same. I always have and always will. Peter is, of course, a busybody with no backbone. He can't stand up to parents. He's always taking their side. Now he's making up stories about me so he can do what the parents want just because it makes his life easier if he doesn't have to resist them. This has been going on for a long time. I hope Peter hasn't fooled you like he did your predecessor." Ms. Barter turns and walks away.

Elizabeth wonders what she should do now. What, if anything, should Peter do?

Discussion

If this were merely a case in which Ms. Barter and the others disagreed about pedagogy, issues of ethics would not arise. It is common for teachers to disagree about educational approaches, and discussions of those disagreements are normal and desirable. Effective schools provide forums for such discussions and reliable procedures for resolving them.

But a significant ethical issue occurs here when Ms. Barter denies to Elizabeth that she ever said the things Peter reported. Here she has lied, and by lying, she has humiliated Peter or at least invited the possibility of such humiliation. That is wrong.

But, of course, there is no way that Elizabeth can prove that Ms. Barter lied since she was not present for the conversation that Peter reported. This is a he-said-she-said situation that presents little opportunity for Elizabeth to take sides, whatever her suspicions may be.

Peter's concerns are genuine and deserve Elizabeth's attention. As a school leader, it is her responsibility to ensure implementation of the school's values. But without reliable evidence that Ms. Barter does in fact treat the students of wealthy parents unfairly, there is little Elizabeth can do beyond calling attention to the school's policies of treating all students fairly. If Peter wishes to pursue this—and feels he has an obligation to do so—his immediate task is to collect whatever evidence he can to support the charge that Ms. Barter discriminates unfairly in her treatment of students. That evidence, if it can be collected, is the *sine qua non* of administrative action here. Without it, members of the school community can only work harder to reinforce for Ms. Barter the school's commitment to fair and equal treatment of all students.

LAPTOP SECRETS

Mario is the assistant technology director at Central High School. He enjoys working with students, but his greatest satisfaction comes from trouble-shooting technical problems. He likes to say, "I've never met a busted laptop I couldn't fix. Never!" The teachers love him because he is always willing to help with their problems, even if he has to stay late at night to do so. They also know that Mario is willing to work on their personal computers although he is only supposed to work on those that are owned by the school.

One day, Allen, a social studies teacher, asks Mario if he can help with the serious problem that is afflicting Allen's personal laptop. Mario, ever the enthusiast, says, "Of course. Bring it on." Allen opens his briefcase and pulls out the laptop. "Mario," he says, "I can't tell you how much I appreciate this."

Mario takes Allen's computer home that night and works on it in the workshop in his basement. He quickly discerns that the problem is just a software startup conflict, nothing major. He reformats the hard drive and eliminates some older versions of software, which seem to fix the problem. To be sure the computer is working, he opens Allen's word processor and chooses the most recent document to test. But he cannot help noticing that the document is in the form of a diary. In it, Allen has written at length of his fantasies about a girl in one of his classes. Much of it is very sexual. As he reads through the entire entry—which goes on for several pages—Mario finds nothing that indicates Allen has acted on these fantasies. Uncertain what, if anything, he will do with this information, Mario decides to print a copy of it.

The next day he returns the repaired laptop to Allen. He wonders what he should do with the information he has printed out.

Discussion

We begin by noting here that, while Mario and Allen are co-workers at school, this case does not directly involve their work in that capacity. The laptop in question was Allen's personal computer, and Mario worked on it as his friend, not as part of his official responsibilities. If the school where they both worked had policies that limited the ways in which school-owned computers could be used and if Mario were working on such a computer as part of his job, significant questions would arise here. Clearly, for a teacher to use a school-owned computer to record sexual fantasies about a student is inappropriate. And if another school employee should encounter that written record in the normal course of school business, some response would be necessary.

That response might take the form of a direct contact with Allen, in which Mario—or whoever discovered the writing—indicated its inappropriateness. And if Allen did not see his actions as questionable or was unwilling to stop, Mario should bring his behavior to the attention of the school principal.

This case is different, however, because the school does not own this computer; there is no evidence that Allen's writing occurred at school. Furthermore, Mario was not working on this computer in any official capacity. Nor—importantly—is there any evidence that Allen had *acted* in an inappropriate way toward the student about whom he was writing or any other student. In a country governed by the First Amendment, citizens are not held to public account for their private writings.

As a friend, Mario might have pointed out to Allen that he had inadvertently come across this document and was troubled by it. He might also have cautioned Allen about its substantive impropriety. But he was wrong to make a copy of it. And he is under no obligation to report his discovery to anyone.

Ethical situations often involve a balance between institutional policies and individual rights. Specific circumstances usually determine where the balance falls (Pellicer, 2003; Strike, 1990). In this case, the private nature of Allen's writings and the nonofficial character of Mario's discovery of them would seem to make this a private matter in which Allen's rights to privacy and freedom of expression ought to prevail.

BLACKBALL

Jim was shocked when he learned that he had not been elected to his high school's Red Key Society (RKS). Jim ranks third in the junior class and 20 members of his class were elected to RKS and would be inducted at a ceremony in two weeks. All of the other students who ranked in the top 10 in the class were among those chosen. Jim was so distraught that he decided to speak with Mr. Mikelson, his advisor. Mikelson was a new science teacher with whom he had a good relationship. His question to the teacher was simple, "What have I done wrong?"

(Continued)

(Continued)

Mr. Mikelson had no good answer. Jim was the best student in his chemistry class and had always seemed diligent, curious, and intellectually engaged. Now in his second year at the school, Mikelson had encountered no better student, so he decided to talk with one of his senior colleagues, Mrs. Adams, about Jim's question. Mrs. Adams had been at the school for more than 20 years, had been an informal mentor to Mikelson in his first year, and had always seemed very fair-minded in his conversations with her.

In that discussion, Mrs. Adams said that membership in RKS was recognition of high academic achievement but that it was not automatic. Character was important, too, and all of the teachers in the school voted on the candidates. The tradition was that any teacher could veto a candidate if he or she had doubts about that person's honesty or integrity. The veto required no explanation.

Mikelson recalled the vote but had no recollection of anyone speaking against Jim; he asked if some teacher had blackballed him. Mrs. Adams said that she had heard in the teacher's lounge that Arlene Sawyer had cast the veto that kept Jim out of RKS. She had not explained her veto at the time selections were made but later told some other teachers that she knew some things about Jim that she had learned when she chaperoned a church camping trip the previous spring that called his character into question and made it impossible for her to support his induction into RKS.

This troubled Mikelson. "How can we allow a teacher to blackball a student without explaining the substance of her reasons for that?" he asked. "And why are teachers permitted to use information—even if it's true—that occurs outside of school time or official school activities? Is it fair to single out one student in this way?"

"I share some of your concerns," Mrs. Adams responded, "but that's just the way we do things here. It's always been our tradition that the vote for membership in the Red Key Society has to be unanimous. I'm sorry Jim is upset about this, but maybe he needs to take some of the responsibility for the behavior that caused one of the teachers to vote against him." Then smiling slyly, Mrs. Adams also said, "Of course, it's also possible that Arlene vetoed him because she's still upset that Jim did not try out for the school play she was directing. He told her playing basketball was more important to him than drama. I know she chose that play with him in mind for the lead, and she was very disappointed when he declined to take part."

The conversation ended with Mikelson more dissatisfied than he was at the beginning and still feeling that Jim was treated unfairly. What, if anything, should he do now?

Discussion

Mikelson is a relatively new teacher at the school, and he has just had a direct encounter with the school's culture. He does not like what he's found. It is not uncommon for new teachers in a school to discover that traditional and time-honored ways of doing things are troubling to them. School culture exerts powerful pressure on school community members' behavior (Barth, 2001). We see this in students' conformity to peers. Certainly veteran teachers who wield power in the larger community can be strong barriers to change. Furthermore, teachers can be inured to somewhat harmful traditions and practices because they are reluctant to examine their effects (Chaleff, 2003; Starratt, 2005). The newcomer who simply asks *why* can be both a breath of fresh air as well as a thorn in the side of the entrenched powers.

But this case raises two kinds of questions. The first is whether the school's culture or policies, at least in this matter, need to be changed. Is it right for a single teacher to be able to prevent the election of a student to the school's honor society? And even if that policy were to be retained, is it right for the vetoing teacher to do so without explanation? Those are matters of policy and presumably there are procedures and venues in this school in which Mikelson can initiate a discussion and review of these policies.

In the substance of this case, there are also ethical issues. Is it right for teachers in the school to judge and reward or punish students for their behavior outside of school? We often assume that a student's behavior and character, as revealed in the confines of the school and during the hours of the school day, are relevant to the way that student is treated. But when such judgments are based on actions or alleged actions that occur outside of school, inevitable problems arise. It is not unusual for schools to punish students who break the law outside of school or who are known to attend parties for school teams where alcohol is consumed even though the parties occur off school property during nonschool hours.

Where is the proper line between actions of students outside of school that deserve some kind of sanction from the school and student behavior that is outside the purview of school officials? There is no simple answer to that question, but it is certainly worthy of discussion. If students are being denied honors they otherwise deserve for reasons that have no direct bearing on their performance or behavior *as students* there ought to be a heavy burden of proof on the teachers or school officials who want to punish them in this way. They ought to be required to explain why such behavior is relevant to the school's decision making about such honors. Certainly the unexplained veto in this situation does not rise to that level of proof.

The more troubling ethical question here is whether, as Mrs. Adams hinted, Arlene Sawyer's veto in this case was not the result of the reasons she stated—Jim's behavior on a church trip—but rather a consequence of her anger at him for not participating in the school play. Students have a right to choose the extracurricular activities in which they desire to participate. Teachers will not always be happy with the choices they make, particularly when those affect the extracurricular activities for which the teacher bears responsibility. But to punish students, directly or indirectly, for exercising their right to make extracurricular choices is clearly wrong. And if Arlene Sawyer vetoed Jim's selection for RKS for that reason, or even if his decision not to participate in the play influenced her veto, she acted unethically.

At a minimum, it would be appropriate and even desirable for Mikelson to speak to Arlene Sawyer about his concerns and to try to determine whether such inappropriate actions occurred. If he concludes that they did, he should ask her to reconsider her vote. If she declines to do so, the next step for Mikelson is to take his concerns to the school council or other relevant decision-making body in order to, at the very least, open up the discussion of the appropriateness of this kind of selection procedure.

Few relationships invite more ethical entanglements than those that involve a teacher's colleagues. In the tight proximity of working relationships in a school, we will sometimes observe actions or choices of colleagues that trouble us. Sometimes those are simply matters of disagreement about policies, but sometimes, too, they involve fundamental principles of ethical behavior.

The difficulty in dealing with these conflicts is compounded by the educational tradition of academic freedom, especially as regards the autonomy of teachers in dealing with their own subject matter and their own students. Teachers are reluctant to question the pedagogy or student interactions of other teachers, and often rightly so. But inevitably, there will be times when one teacher will see in the actions of another teacher something that seems wrong. In responding to that, it is well to review the troubling action in the light of some of the principles and decision rules outlined at the beginning of this book to help determine whether it does, in fact, raise serious ethical questions.

If it does, then the observing teacher must determine a strategy for response. The responses will vary depending on the substance of the troubling action and the personalities and procedures that exist in the school (Keith-Spiegel, Whitley, Balogh, Perkins, & Wittig, 2002).

But a failure to respond when a teacher believes a colleague has committed a serious ethical violation is itself unethical. All teachers bear collective responsibility for the ethical standards of their school, and silence or inaction in response to an observed ethical violation compounds the impact of the violation on the school community. It cannot be justified.

For Reflection and Conversation

The following are cases similar to the ones presented in this chapter. How would you analyze the individual's obligations and what might be appropriate next steps for the teachers to take?

❖ ❖ ❖

1. John teaches history at a middle school, and he and Martha, a language arts teacher, were assigned by the principal to prepare for the school's Civil Rights Day Celebration. When John approached Martha to begin the planning, she indicated that she had no interest in this, did not know why she was assigned to do it, and thought that it was really a responsibility for history teachers, not English teachers. She also said she was busy with "other things in her life" and had no time to work on the project. John is a young teacher who does not yet have tenure. He worries that if the celebration is not well planned, a negative evaluation might result. So he does all the planning himself.

The celebration is a big success, and when it is over the principal calls John and Martha up on stage to congratulate them for their good work. Martha happily accepts his congratulations. John later wonders if he should indicate to the principal that Martha did none of the work or perhaps if he should say something to Martha about this. What do you think?

2. Last week, we were interviewing for a special education position in my elementary school. There were two finalists. One of them currently works part-time at our school, generally one day a week. I have worked with her on a few occasions and have found her cooperative, helpful, and creative. But she is a very quiet person and did not interview well. The others on the interview team, none of whom had ever worked directly with her, were not impressed.

The other candidate was a much better interviewee. He was confident, self-possessed, and full of good ideas. He also had more experience, having held a similar full-time position at a school not unlike ours. When I mentioned the interviews to my husband over dinner that night, he asked the name of the second candidate. When I told him, he responded immediately, "Oh you don't want that guy. He used to work at my school—before I came. I've heard a lot about him. Every time his name came up, teachers would say he is the laziest person they'd ever worked with."

This left me wondering whether it was appropriate for me to discuss these interviews with my husband who is a teacher, though not in the school where I work. Should I have said anything about the interviews? Should I have revealed the name of a candidate under consideration? And what, if anything, should I do with the information my husband has given me? Should I share that with my colleagues on the interview team?

3. One of my colleagues is in trouble. I'm not sure of the cause, but I have recently observed enough examples of erratic behavior to indicate that something is seriously wrong. I don't know whether he is drinking, using drugs, or suffering some kind of mental illness. Nor do I know him very well; we're not friends. But we are colleagues in the same department, we attend department meetings together, and we have to work together on curriculum and other issues. I find it increasingly difficult to work with him because he is often late for meetings, or leaves meetings and returns later, or says things at meetings that seem irrational.

I've discussed this with some of my other colleagues and we are in agreement that something is wrong. But we don't know what to do. Should we conduct an "intervention" and confront the colleague whose behavior worries us? Should we report it to the principal and leave the problem to her, even though that may affect evaluations and perhaps the continued employment of our colleague? Or should we do nothing because this is a personal matter and not our professional responsibility?

4. One afternoon, a student whom you know well and whose integrity is beyond question comes to talk to you about a personal problem. He asks you to keep the conversation in confidence, and you agree to do so, not knowing what its subject will be.

He begins by talking hypothetically about a friend and how he is troubled by his friend's actions. Before long, it is apparent that the friend is well known to both of you, as is the other principal figure in the discussion. This is no longer a matter of hypotheticals or anonymous persons.

The issues are these: The friend in question is a student who is a high school senior and 18 years old. The student is engaged in a romantic relationship with a faculty member in whose English class he is now enrolled. The teacher in question is a member of the English department that you chair.

Several students, having suspected this relationship and in a kind of intervention, confronted the student. The student confessed to his participation in the relationship.

The student who discusses this with you has several concerns. First, he is concerned that his friend is making a serious mistake by allowing this relationship to occur. Second, he is disturbed that his friend does not see the impropriety of the relationship nor the danger that it poses for him and for the teacher. Third, he is frustrated by his own inability, despite good faith efforts, to help his friend avoid the problems this entanglement poses.

The student came to you out of frustration and is not asking you to take any particular action, just to listen to his concerns and reflect on them. In fact, he expresses some concern that if some action were taken against the teacher or student involved in the relationship, he would quickly be recognized as the "rat" who revealed the relationship and would be ostracized by his friends. He thanks you for listening to him but asks you not to tell anyone what you've heard. What, if anything, do you do now?

6

The Sum of the Parts

Teachers on Collaborative Teams

The concept of the school as a series of one-room schoolhouses where teachers have neither time nor inclination to share much beyond their plans for the weekend has been challenged lately by the growing acceptance of the desirability of collaboration, teamwork, and collegial learning (Wei, Darling-Hammond, Andree, Richardson, & Orphanos, 2009). Schools are rapidly adopting the philosophy that teachers and schools benefit from collaborative work (DuFour, Eaker, & DuFour, 2005). The advantages of this team approach are several. Teams can divide the labor, allowing each member to do what he or she does best. In that sense, a team can be more than the sum of its parts. Teamwork also contributes to inspiration and innovation. By sharing ideas, by brainstorming, individual members of the team have access to ideas and approaches they might not have considered or known about on their own.

Teams also enhance collective efficacy, individual members' beliefs that the group is more effective because of the contributions of each member (Bandura, 1986; Goddard, Hoy, & Woolfolk-Hoy, 2000). No one wants to let the team down. The team approach can be especially valuable for younger teachers because it provides them opportunities to work closely with and to observe first hand their more experienced colleagues as long as the climate allows them to pose naïve questions about taken-for-granted assumptions and tradition-bound practices (Bryk & Schneider, 2002).

In spite of the many benefits, working closely with other adults in mutually dependent relationships can pose problems for teachers. Because they are no longer isolated from each other, they learn more about the teachers in their school and may discover how much their teaching practices and teaching philosophies differ (Ackerman & Mackenzie, 2007; Barth, 2006). Because teacher collaboration is connected to the core of the school's work—student learning—accountability measures highlight these differences and allow for judgments about effectiveness. What often becomes clear as well is that teachers are much more skilled at working with students than with their own colleagues. No one has expected them either to be good colleagues or to learn how to be effective "critical" friends (Donaldson, 2006). So it is not surprising that such groups often encounter difficulties, many of which revolve around the interactions between individual team members. Teams are groups of individuals who may have different educational philosophies, varying levels of commitment and diligence, and a range of social skills (Johnson & Johnson, 2005). Blending personalities and differences can be a challenge to any team.

Perhaps the most common difficulty confronting a team occurs when some members of the team feel that other members are not doing their share of the work or contributing an appropriate level of thought and creativity to the team's joint efforts. If a member of the team regularly comes late to meetings or misses them altogether, does not follow through on assignments, treats others in the group with disrespect, or fails to preserve the confidentiality of team discussions, other members have to decide how to respond. It is never simple to determine an appropriate response to the team member who is not a team player.

As much as educators may be schooled in team development, going carefully through the convening and contracting stages (Donaldson & Sanderson, 1996), they can quickly resort to paths of least resistance when it comes to attending to and reminding each other of their established ground rules. The weakest or loudest member of the group may become dominant because it is easier for other members to go along than to resist. In addition, teams sometimes become overly protective of their members and fail to respond appropriately when one of them acts in ways the others do not like. All teams inevitably acquire norms of performance and standards of ethical behavior. Team members are often at a loss, though, when one of them violates those standards. If a teacher on the team gives an undeserved passing grade to a student who happens to live in her neighborhood, how should the other team members respond? Should they stand behind their team member even if they disapprove of her behavior?

Should they directly challenge her actions? Should they report her violation of professional ethics to an administrator? Those are difficult questions, and some of them will be addressed in the cases that follow.

Collaborative teams benefit from open discussion of ethical issues. We have noted throughout this book that consultation is an important first response whenever an individual in a school confronts an ethical dilemma. And in nearly every way the collaborative team of which a teacher is a member is a good and appropriate place to have those consultative discussions. Such discussions can serve two purposes. First, they can help individual teachers decide how to act when faced with an ethical quandary by offering the shared wisdom and experience of other group members. Second, they can contribute to the group's definition and refinement of its own ethical culture, so that when members of the group are confronted with ethical challenges in the future, they will have a more sophisticated understanding of how to respond.

Developing the ethical culture of the team ought to be regarded as an important component of team building. Explicit consideration of ethical issues, both in the abstract and when they arise in practical situations, can help team members sharpen their ethical sensitivities and better meet their ethical obligations.

DOUBLE TEAM

Barbara had been teaching at a suburban elementary school for three years. She had been out of teaching for nearly a decade before that while she stayed home to concentrate on raising her three children. When she and her husband divorced, she needed an independent income and returned to teaching full-time. She is a member of a collaborative team of five people who teach a variety of subjects. Teams play an important role in defining and implementing the curriculum in her school.

The leader of Barbara's team is Marcia, a language arts teacher who has been at the school for more than 20 years. Marcia is highly regarded both by her colleagues on the team and broadly among the faculty. One of the reasons the team has worked so well is Marcia's diligent effort to engage each of the team members in its collective efforts. But recently she has begun to worry about the contributions of Arthur, a math teacher. Arthur is about the same age as Barbara and, like her, was divorced a few years ago. Arthur has never been the most enthusiastic member of the team; indeed, Marcia has often had cause to worry about whether Arthur really believed in the collaborative team approach to curriculum development and teaching. But she has been able to nudge and cajole him to be a pretty reliable team member.

(Continued)

(Continued)

But over the past few months, Marcia has noticed that Barbara seems to be doing a lot of the work assigned to Arthur, even drafting the section of the team's annual planning report that was his responsibility. Neither of them said Barbara had done so, but it was very clear to a veteran language teacher like Marcia that the same person had written the sections assigned to Barbara and Arthur. After observing the two of them at team meetings and in other settings in the school, Marcia had come to believe that Barbara was romantically interested in Arthur and was expressing that interest by taking on much of the work that he should have been doing. It was unclear whether Arthur shared that romantic interest, but he seemed happy that someone else was willing to do the work in which he had little interest.

Though she was unhappy that Arthur was contributing so little to the team, she had to admit to herself that the joint work of the team had improved since Barbara was doing much of Arthur's share as well as her own. In a way, this pleased Marcia because, as a team leader, her annual evaluations are affected by the performance of her team. But she also has responsibility for the operations of her team, and she could not overlook the declining participation and contributions of Arthur. She wondered whether she should simply let things continue as they were or directly express her concerns to Barbara and Arthur, both of whom might react negatively to her meddling in their personal relationship.

What should Marcia do?

Discussion

It might be easy in this situation for Marcia to take an "if-it-ain't-broke-don't-fix-it" attitude. The work of the group is progressing and the quality of its products is apparently satisfactory. But as the group leader, Marcia has an obligation to superintend its processes as well as its products. One of the primary reasons for establishing collaborative groups is to fully engage each individual member and each individual member's skills and talents in the collaboration.

In this case, Arthur seems to be distancing himself from the group by relying on Barbara to fulfill his responsibilities. If we apply the ethical principle of universality—that is, would it be right if everyone did it—it is clear that Arthur's behavior falls well below an acceptable standard. It is wrong because he is not contributing proportionately or appropriately to the collective work of the group. It is wrong because the group is not benefiting from Arthur's ideas and insights. And it is wrong because, whatever the reason, Arthur is taking advantage of Barbara.

One can certainly imagine that there might be times when a group member is ill, preoccupied with a personal or professional problem, or unable to perform fully the work of a group member. At those times, other members of the group naturally take on a larger share of the responsibilities. That, in fact, is a powerful argument for the collaborative approach in schools. But none of those justifications exist in this case. Arthur is simply failing in his responsibilities as a group member. He has been able to get away with that because of Barbara's willingness to take up the slack.

As the group leader, Marcia has a responsibility to deal with this situation. To minimize defensiveness and embarrassment, an appropriate first step is to speak directly to Arthur. Marcia should describe her observations of the group dynamic and let him know how his participation should change. Her goal here is to enhance his understanding of his individual obligation to be an active collaborator in group activities and decisions.

If this conversation fails to alter Arthur's behavior in a significant way, then Marcia's next step is a conversation with Barbara. Here, too, she should describe her observations of the group dynamic and explain why she thinks it is wrong for Barbara to be doing work assigned to Arthur. She need not get into questions of Barbara's motivations for this but rather focus the discussion on the goals and needs of the group.

Barbara needs to understand that, whatever her motivation, she is violating an important principle: Everyone in a professional setting is responsible for performing his or her own obligations and it is deceitful to take credit for something one has not actually done. By doing Arthur's work for him, Barbara is contributing to the deceit and violating the ethical norms that prevail in any collaborative group. The ethical impropriety of her behavior here is not very different from what it would be if she were to prepare Arthur's lesson plans or grade his students' papers. One might even draw an analogy to a student copying another's homework or plagiarizing a paper. Doing a colleague's work and allowing him to take credit for that is wrong. Barbara needs to understand that. Arthur needs to understand that. And, as the team leader, Marcia is obligated to be certain that both of them understand that.

FOCUSING ON THE GOAL

Everyone at Highland High School was excited when the school won the big grant from a national foundation. It was an honor in itself to win a grant in intense competition, but especially pleasing to most of the faculty at the school was the fact that the grant would support a new approach for which many of them had long yearned. The grant would permit the school to hire two professional consultants, experts in the work of collaborative teams who would guide Highland for two years in its effort to convert its curriculum and faculty organization to collaborative teamwork.

One of the conditions of the grant was that the program at Highland be closely monitored and carefully evaluated. The performance of each team would be assessed each quarter based largely on predetermined measures of student achievement. The instructional strategies of those teams whose students improved most significantly on these measures would be used as models for other teams in the school.

The foundation believed that each school is unique and that no single model of collaborative teamwork would necessarily work well in every school. To find an appropriate model for a particular school, the foundation believed, the best approach was to let the teachers in that school develop their own team approaches and then contrast them with each other to see which worked best. When the most effective teams were identified, then the members of those teams would become facilitators to help other teams adopt their successful approaches. As facilitators, those faculty members would be given course-release time and a significant stipend.

At the end of the first year of the grant, the performance of one team's students had improved far more significantly than any of the others. Even the lowest performing students among those assigned to this team seemed to be making remarkable progress. This was especially noteworthy because students had been randomly assigned to the teams to try to equalize the skills of each team's student load.

Dennis was one of the teachers on that successful team. He was proud of the performance of his team, and he looked forward to its continuation in the second year of the grant so that he could become a facilitator and enjoy the benefits that came with that role. But it did worry Dennis that some of the work of his team seemed to fall outside the parameters established by the grant. Notably, the grant protocols were instituted to ensure that the teaching practices selected were available to and accepted by all teachers and in keeping with the teacher contract.

But Dennis's team had been holding special study nights on Wednesday evenings at the YMCA and half-day "learning picnics" at MacDonald's on the last Saturday of every month. Students were often cajoled into attending. At these sessions, students worked individually with members of the team on their assignments. Team members willingly participated in these out-of-school activities because they were all committed to the success of their team.

> On the one hand, Dennis worried that he was participating in inappropriate activities that violated the conditions of the grant. But, on the other, he was excited about the work of his team and felt that one of the benefits of the collaborative team approach was that it inspired faculty to go above and beyond what was normally expected of them in meeting the needs of their students. If this was one of the outcomes of the grant and the new collaborative approach it sought to encourage, why should he worry or complain about that? After all, he reasoned, his team was definitely improving student performance. Dennis decided that the long-term benefits outweighed any concerns he might have about the short-term impacts on the grant's assessment procedures and that he would not express those concerns to anyone.
>
> Was he right?

Discussion

Among the most difficult ethical dilemmas in a school setting are the conflicts that occur between abiding by the rules and maximizing student learning opportunities. It sometimes occurs, as it does in this case, that teacher efforts to improve learning violate the expectations agreed to by the faculty and school board.

Dennis's actions in this case are especially problematic because there is reason to believe that his behavior is motivated by more than just the desire to improve student learning. Since the grant promises individual benefits to members of the most successful teams—course relief and stipends—an objective observer could reasonably conclude that the desire to receive those individual benefits is an important part of the motivation for Dennis and his team.

Since Dennis and his team have violated the "experimental" protocols of the research design implemented under the grant, it is essential to ask whether the end justifies the means. Has the team acted outside the rules for some purpose of such significance and value that it justifies their behavior? Heroic teachers, portrayed in films and novels, always go above and beyond the requirements of their jobs, throwing themselves into the lives of their students and working long hours, often at great sacrifice to their own personal lives. That happens in real life, too.

One could characterize the behavior of Dennis's group in that way and find it laudable. But the problem here is that in acting this way the group has undermined the conditions established by the foundation for the implementation of the grant. And, in so doing, it has violated the school's commitments when it accepted the grant. Troublesome as well is the possibility that, in acting this way, members of the group were motivated by the possibility of individual rewards, not simply by the desire to improve the learning of their students.

A better approach for Dennis's group would have been to suggest at the outset of the experiment that its approach, including the Wednesday night and weekend meetings, be one of the models tested. Of course, they would have to discuss whether such a model fit within the parameters of the foundation's guidelines. But for the team to proceed on its own with a collaborative approach that violates the protocols established in the grant cannot be justified in this case. The motives of the team members are suspect, but even if they were not, the ends here do not justify the means. It is much more important for the grant consultants to be able to fairly compare appropriate approaches to collaborative efforts and then to implement the best of those for the long term than it is for Dennis's group to proceed outside the rules with behavior that might have significant short-term benefits but not be a reasonable or possible approach to adopt schoolwide.

LUCK OF THE DRAW

Lucy and Donna, a social studies teacher and a language arts teacher, respectively, at Bayside Middle School, had been teaching together for more than a decade. They were part of a team of five teachers that also included a reading, math, and science teacher. During each spring break for the past five years, they had organized a trip to Washington, D.C., for their students. The hotel where they normally stayed could accommodate 40 students, the two teachers, and two other chaperones. This number provided a good ratio of adults to middle schoolers. But this year, there were 50 students who wanted to go on the trip and, though they tried in a number of ways to make arrangements for all to go, it could not be arranged.

Lucy and Donna discussed this problem at their team meeting and decided the only fair way to distribute the 40 slots for the trip was to have a lottery. They would put all the students' names in a box and draw them out in front of the class. A few mornings later during advisory period, Lucy and Donna gathered all the students in the activity room and began drawing names from a box. Lucy and Donna alternated drawing names while students cheered as their names were called. When 39 names had been drawn, 11 remained in contention for the final spot. Lucy reached into the box, pulled out a piece of paper, paused for a second, looked around the room, and read the name of Aaron, one of the best students in their classes. She then put the piece of paper in her pocket, congratulated all the students who were going, and commiserated with those who were not. She promised that she and Donna would find a way to compensate those who could not go on the trip with another activity later on in the spring.

Donna wondered why Lucy had stuck the last name drawn into her pocket rather than into the envelope in which the names of the other chosen students had been placed. When Lucy turned away to speak to one of the selected students who had questions about the logistics of the trip, Donna looked into the box of names of students who were not selected and spotted a piece of paper with Aaron's name on it. She then looked at the other names and realized that Ian's name was missing, even though he stood among the 10 students who were not chosen.

Ian came from a difficult family and was often in trouble. He was not a strong student and was often hard to manage in class. In fact, at the team meeting that preceded the drawing, the members had discussed whether special provisions would be necessary to control Ian if he were chosen for the trip. Donna realized then what had happened: Lucy had drawn Ian's name for the last slot on the trip but had acted as if she had drawn Aaron. To hide the evidence, she put the slip of paper bearing Ian's name in her pocket rather than in the envelope.

Donna's first reaction was relief at not having to worry about Ian on the trip and gratitude for Lucy's clever solution to the problem. But as she thought about this later in the day, she began to contemplate the ethical implications of what had happened that morning and wondered if she should speak to Lucy or the other members of the team.

What should she do now?

Discussion

A simple question casts a harsh light on Lucy's action here: Would it be acceptable if it were widely known what she had done? Earlier, we called this the rule of publicity. One test of the propriety of an action or decision, however desirable its intentions or impacts, is whether it could be justified to a wider public. Could Lucy properly explain her name shifting to all of the students in the class, to their parents, to other teachers, and especially to Ian's parents?

Lucy engaged in deceit. She told the students that a lottery would afford them all an equal opportunity to go on the trip but then did not deliver on her promise. That she was well intentioned is irrelevant in determining the ethical propriety of her actions. If she did not believe that Ian was a suitable student to take on this trip and if others on her team agreed with her, then she should have found some way to inform Ian and his family directly that his teachers did not feel that he was a good candidate for the trip. That is a reasonable decision for a teacher and a collaborative team to make.

But reaching that end through unethical means cannot be justified. Lucy's doing this on her own without consulting Donna or other members of the team simply compounds the impropriety. Now she has put her colleagues in the difficult position of having to stand by her unethical actions or to challenge them in ways that are certain to lead to someone's embarrassment or humiliation. Lucy's decision to call Aaron's name may have been spontaneous and unplanned. But that makes it no less wrong.

A difficult burden falls on Donna in this case since she alone knows about Lucy's unethical action. Her first responsibility is to speak to Lucy and tell her that she knows what occurred and that she expects Lucy to take corrective action. If Lucy declines to do so, then Donna should take her concerns to the full team for discussion. If, on the other hand, Lucy realizes that she has done something wrong, it may be helpful and prudent as well for her to get the advice of the team in correcting her error.

If no corrective steps are taken, the situation is aggravated even further. To fail to admit and seek to correct unethical activity implicitly condones it. Lucy and Donna both have obligations here to seek a cure for the problems Lucy has created. And if other members of the team are informed of these problems, they too share the burden of seeking an appropriate course of correction.

THE FRUSTRATED VICTIM

Tom had had enough. He was the lead teacher of a department at City High School. He had long believed that their students performed effectively because of the extraordinary talents of the members. The intellectual leader of the group was Mark, who taught psychology and was much beloved by current and past students. Although he had a doctorate in psychology and had taught at a college for a few years, he decided he preferred teaching high school students.

Mark was a valuable contributor to the work of the team, often suggesting creative approaches to the curriculum and the use of class time. Tom and Mark had worked together for years and had become good friends. So it was extremely difficult for Tom when, as lead teacher, he had to confront the problem of Mark's hostility toward another teacher, Annie.

Annie had come to the school a year earlier. In the first year, all the team members were welcoming and helpful to Annie. She encountered many of the normal difficulties that confront first-year teachers, and the members of the team had tried to be as supportive as they could in helping her manage. By the end of the year, she seemed to have found her footing and her confidence bloomed. Her second year was much better.

But Tom had begun to notice the dynamic of department meetings changing. It seemed as if every time Annie suggested something, Mark shot it down. Sometimes he would say, "Oh we've already tried that." Other times when

Annie suggested a new initiative, Mark would say, "I think our students are way beyond that." And more recently Mark seemed to respond to many of Annie's comments with a dismissive snicker. Annie was the only female member of the department, and Mark treated none of the male members the same way.

Tom decided to talk to Annie about this and, when he did, she began to cry. "Thank you for noticing," she said to Tom. "I feel like Mark hates me, or he hates women, and I can't do anything about it. I'm new, and he's been here a long time. I just graduated from college, and he has a doctorate. And maybe he's right; maybe my ideas and suggestions aren't very good. Now I find myself just keeping quiet when there's something I want to contribute because I know how Mark will respond."

After Tom offered some supportive comments, he suggested that she speak to Mark directly about her concerns. "I did," Annie quickly responded. "I spoke to him after school about a month ago saying exactly what I just told you, that I felt he was belittling me perhaps because I'm a woman. He said I was crazy, that he thought it was his responsibility to disagree with anyone's ideas if he thought they were wrong. Then I reminded him that he never disagreed with any of the men on the team. He said that was because the men always seem to have good ideas."

"So you don't think that accomplished anything," said Tom.

"Worse," said Annie. "It convinced me even more that Mark would never take me seriously because I'm a woman."

"Would you like me to speak to Mark about this?" Tom asked.

"No, I doubt it would do any good," said Annie. "He would just think that I was spreading stories about him to destroy his reputation. I think what I'll do is ask for a transfer to another school. I don't think Mark will ever accept me as an equal member of this group."

As Tom thought about this conversation, he was troubled. Not only did he like and respect Annie, he thought she had the potential to be an excellent teacher and a valuable member of the school. But the dynamic of the group had changed since she joined it and in ways that made it collectively less effective. If she were to leave the department, its performance might well improve. On the other hand, he could not approve of or acquiesce to Mark's behavior, but he was not certain what, if anything, he could do about it.

What advice would you give to Tom in this situation?

Discussion

Tom faces a difficult conflict. On the one hand, if Annie leaves the department, its performance might well improve, and Tom's work as the lead teacher might be simplified. On the other hand, Annie's departure will represent a failure of Tom's leadership, and it will appear to condone Mark's inappropriate attitude toward Annie and perhaps toward women generally.

If Tom does nothing and Annie moves to another school, two kinds of harm will occur. First, one of the essential purposes of working in collaborative teams will have been violated. Collaborative teams are seen as a mechanism for integrating new faculty members into the work and culture of the school and providing them with a support network as they wrestle with the natural difficulties of young teachers learning to succeed (Fullan & Hargreaves, 1996). Clearly, Tom's group has failed to serve that purpose, and if Tom does nothing, the failure is unmitigated.

Second, Mark has acted here in ways that violate fundamental community values. No school can prosper if teachers fail to respect each other for reasons that have to do with race, religion, gender, or any other similar characteristic (Plante, 2004). If Mark genuinely believes that Annie's ideas lack merit, there are certainly ways to express that without humiliating her. But to both Annie and Tom, it appears that Mark's reactions are rooted in sexism more than substance. For Tom and the rest of the department to permit that to go unchallenged would also be a significant failure of responsibility to protect the values of the school community.

Tom should speak directly to Mark, explaining his observations of the interaction between Mark and Annie. He should be sure to note that he is not simply expressing Annie's frustrations but his own as well. In this conversation, Tom should identify specific instances in which Mark's reaction to Annie seems inappropriate. If Mark continues to argue that his criticisms of Annie's ideas are solely substantive and that he has no intention of changing his behavior, then Tom should take further action. He might first consult with other members of the team to see if they regard Mark's actions in the same light as Tom does. He might further suggest that other members speak to Mark.

Mark's attitude is a school problem, not just a department problem. And if it cannot be resolved within the team, a different approach that engages the supervising administrator will be necessary. But the best solution will come from within the group. This school is on the road to a less hierarchical approach to school organization. Rather than revert to less professional socialization (Sergiovanni, 1992), it is imperative for Tom to be transparent about his concerns in the team so that dialogue about his observations can be a renorming as well as a true learning experience. The goal here is to "transform teachers from subordinates to self-managers [because] these strategies are also well-matched to the complex behaviors in good teaching and learning" (Segiovanni, 1992, p. 97). Teachers' moral courage is required to ensure the full advancement of schools as safe and solid institutions for all participants.

Teachers' work increasingly involves collegial and collaborative interactions with others. Close knowledge of others' actions and dispositions can exacerbate the tension between maintaining relationships and critiquing others' teaching practice and professionalism. It is important to avoid polarizing people by immediately pointing out ethical breaches; nevertheless, all teachers must take seriously their responsibilities not just to students in the classrooms but to the tenor of relationships with each other as they go about the business of school.

For Reflection and Conversation

The following cases are similar to those already presented in this chapter. How would you analyze the individual's obligations, and what might be appropriate next steps for the teachers to take?

❖ ❖ ❖

1. A few years ago, Peter and Jim were part of a summer institute on middle-level teaming promoted by a new principal. They became a two-person teaching team because, fortunately, Jim was certified in science and math and Peter in social studies and language arts. They and a core of other teachers were responsible for bringing true middle school principles to the school. After a few years, they were so successful that the school won a state award and a large grant to "scale up" their work. The principal's goal was to ensure that all teams followed a middle school philosophy and that all teams—no matter what their size—worked together planning appropriate instruction for their students.

Peter and Jim were enthusiastic about the reform agenda until they realized that the plan necessitated their splitting up. Some teachers were reluctant to follow the program, and the principal saw Peter and Jim as leaders who could get everyone on board. Peter and Jim were not eager to assume this role and asserted that their partnership was working: They had test results and parent satisfaction data to prove it, and they felt their partnership should continue. Peter and Jim argued that, although they had been a "well-oiled" machine for a few years now, they still had things to learn from each other that could make their collaboration even more effective. Couldn't they just do demonstrations for the other faculty members? Other teachers were welcome to ask them any questions, visit their classrooms, and use their lesson plans. What the principal was proposing would result in a "regression toward the mean," no pockets of excellence to hold out as exemplars of true middle school teaching.

When the principal came to them and told them of her intention to assign them to lead two different teams, Peter and Jim declined to do so, explaining that they had met their responsibilities by developing the team concept for their school and it was now the responsibility of others to implement it. Did they act properly here? What further action, if any, should the principal take?

2. While helping John, a fellow English teacher, move into a new room and a new assignment, Susan discovered that he had a stockpile of multiple class sets of text books, e.g., 100 copies of *The Grapes of Wrath, The Great Gatsby,* and *the Adventures of Huckleberry Finn.* There were more books than she or any other member of their department had been able to obtain even though some of those they were using were very dilapidated and the students and their parents complained about them constantly. John had apparently been "working the system" to secure this number of texts while all the English teachers had been asked to cut budgets and, in some cases, to eliminate new book requests altogether. For years, the English department chair had told the members of the department that they could not purchase new sets of books; they could only order replacement copies of texts they were using, but no more than 25 of each, enough for one class at a time.

Susan found no evidence that John had cheated or lied, only that he had worked through personal contacts at the school system's central finance office to get around the English department's restrictions for the benefit of his own students.

Is it ethical for a teacher to work outside department policies even if ostensibly the purpose is to improve the learning opportunities for his students? How should Susan deal with her discovery?

3. At a meeting for a third-grade student whose disabilities required only reasonable accommodation—a 504 plan—Rick is the only teacher from the team who showed up. None of the others had told him that they would not be present, each assuming that he or she would be the only one absent. How should Rick deal with this? What does he say to the parents? Is it right to make excuses for the teachers, even if they are inventions, in order to prevent the parents from being angry at this apparent lack of interest in the welfare of their child?

4. No one on his team considered Harold a team player. Fellow teachers did not think of him as a solid member of the school community. He ignored collective responsibilities from small things like never retrieving announcements from his mailbox to larger things like correcting papers during Sustained Silent Reading (SSR). He was intimidating, too. If another teacher brought up any directive he ignored or suggested that he participate in meetings more fully, he snapped off a sarcastic comment about not being paid to do anything but teach math. Simply put, Harold was a noncontributing and unpleasant team member. And, to some members, it appeared that he was consciously trying to undermine the collaborative effectiveness of the team to prove his long-standing argument that collaborative teams are educational nonsense. What approaches would you recommend to other members of the team in dealing with the problem he poses to their collective work?

7

Clash of Philosophies

The School Faculty

Relations between individual teachers and the faculties on which they serve pose some of the most complicated ethical challenges in a school setting. Teachers have dual roles, and they are often in conflict. On the one hand, they are employees with obligations to comply with policies, follow the instructions of supervisors, and abide by contractual provisions. On the other, teachers are educational professionals with well-honed personal philosophies and strong beliefs about pedagogy.

Problems arise when the former conflicts with the latter. When teachers find that the school's policies or procedures—whether determined by their colleagues, administrators, or a lay board—directly conflict with their individual views or values, they confront a difficult dilemma. Should they comply with those policies or instructions or resist them? And if they choose to resist them or to challenge them, what are the appropriate ways to do that?

Rare indeed is the teacher who at some point in a career does not confront this dilemma. Balancing personal philosophies with school policies or other professionals' views is a constant challenge, one that every teacher should be prepared to meet with a thoughtful understanding of the proper balance between the individual and the school community (Berlak & Berlak, 1981; Sizer & Sizer, 1999).

TRYING TO GET UNTRACKED

After Dorothea returned from spring break, she was informed by the principal of Eagle Heights School that the administration had decided, without any kind of consultation with her or the other language arts teachers, that they would institute a reading class in the fall for struggling readers. Because Dorothea was the only person on staff with a degree in literacy, she was told that she would teach the course.

This directive was deeply unsettling to Dorothea. She was angry because she knew in her heart that this kind of class would be viewed as remedial and simply another track in an already tracked school. She was also upset with the process: The head of the school assumed he could simply create this program and dump it in Dorthea's lap without ever talking to her or the other members of the English department.

Dorothea arranged a meeting with the principal and the curriculum coordinator and argued her case. She told them that she thought there were serious literacy issues in the school but that simply creating a remedial reading class was a Band-Aid, not a cure. She reminded them that struggling readers were already placed with teachers who had a pretty good sense of how to help them and that there would be little value added in the reading class they had proposed.

She presented them with a plan for a literacy initiative that she thought was much more promising than the addition of a reading class. Her initiative involved appointing or hiring a literacy coach to be the facilitator of a literacy program and a consultant to the school faculty. This, she argued, would be the basis for the professional development of all teachers who in turn would be better able to address low literacy levels of students in their classes. Her professional opinion was that literacy improvements are much more likely to come when students work in familiar settings with their regular teachers than when they are placed in reading classes that might well be unfamiliar to them and a source of stigma because their very assignment to those classes labels them as poor readers.

Two weeks later, the principal told Dorothea that they were taking her proposal under advisement and had dropped the reading class idea for now. Dorothea heard nothing more about this until the next spring when the curriculum coordinator announced at a faculty meeting that they were adopting a literacy-across-the-curriculum program. In addition, they were creating a class for struggling readers and would hire a literacy coach to teach this class and to work with teachers to help them incorporate literacy strategies in classrooms. Dorothea was pleased that the plan seemed to reflect her view that the school needed a broad literacy initiative; at the same time, though, she was distressed that the administration had not abandoned its initial plan for a separate reading class and the continued tracking of students which it required and which she strongly opposed.

Dorothea had long had a reputation at the school as an opponent of tracking and she was proud of it. She talked about the situation in a graduate class in which she was enrolled at the university. "The revolutionary in me rebels at this structure," she told the class. "I had made my case against this class based on the principle that further tracking would be counterproductive to democratic classrooms. When I've talked to my colleagues about pedagogies of revolution, social justice, and love, they look at me like I've lost my mind."

When she met with the administrators again to reiterate her unhappiness about the separate remedial reading class, she was told that the class was going to happen. They agreed that a shift in faculty thinking and teaching needed to happen, but that such a shift would take time. In the short term, they intended to create the reading class they originally proposed to help the students with the most difficult literacy challenges and that she would teach it.

Dorothea now faced some difficult choices. Should she simply comply with the decisions made by the administrators and teach the class she had opposed? Should she express her opposition to other teachers in her department and the school in an effort to stir up opposition to the administration's plan? Should she resign from the faculty in protest against a policy that conflicted with her professional judgment and pedagogical philosophy?

Discussion

At the root of this case is a disagreement in values between the school administrators and Dorothea. Her professional values are in conflict with theirs, so they have arrived at different conclusions about how to handle the literacy achievement challenges in their school. It will be useful for Dorothea to understand this as she sorts out her own options. It seems unlikely that she will be able to convince the school administrators that their approach is wrong and hers is right.

She is certainly entitled to talk with other teachers to see if they share her views and a similar degree of passion. If she finds that they do, it would not be inappropriate for them to express some collective judgment to the school administrators in support of the position that Dorothea has taken throughout this discussion. But in following this approach Dorothea takes a risk, what we might describe as a political risk. By extending this discussion beyond what the administrators believe is a final decision point, she will irritate them—perhaps even anger them—to the extent that they will be less willing to consult with her in the future on policy matters regarding literacy. Like anyone confronting a difficult situation of this sort, Dorothea needs to balance short-term and long-term goals and opportunities.

Any teacher, faced with a distasteful policy, has the option to resign. Exercising that option has significant practical consequences in terms of income and future professional opportunities. For most teachers, a resignation in protest of a school policy would normally be a last resort and one that would be taken only in the most extreme circumstances.

Resignation would appear to be an overreaction for Dorothea in this case. She opposes an aspect of the school's new literacy policy, but she should also understand that her views were heard, apparently taken into consideration, and implemented in part. That is to say that the process of decision making, at least eventually, was consultative. Her opposition to tracking was expressed and considered. But she has been working in a school which for some time has been tracking students, so to participate in the new program would be a change perhaps in degree but not in kind.

Most people work in settings that are governed by policies that they do not support in every aspect. As long as there are internal opportunities to express concern or disagreement with those policies and to seek to change them in the future, employees generally make their peace with their work environment. That is Dorothea's situation here.

She might also note that a resignation in protest, which might have significant and negative personal and professional consequences for her, would do little to change the policies of her school. In fact, her departure from that school might strengthen the position of those who favored the tracking that she opposed. So she has to ask herself: How heavily do my pedagogical values weigh in the choices I face? Do I feel that the proposed remedial reading class is such an affront to my beliefs that I can longer work in a school that is creating such class? If the only answer to those questions is yes, then perhaps resigning from the school is the right choice for Dorothea.

But if the conflict between her personal values and the school's policies is not this black and white, then Dorothea should not resign and instead should participate in the implementation of the policy, seeking openly to shape it to comport as closely as possible with her views on the most effective ways to help students who face literacy challenges.

TEACHING AND FREEDOM

It was his eleventh year of teaching, and Mark could not remember a single week in that time that had passed without frustration. It was not frustration with the daily challenges of teaching; he loved those. Nor was it frustration with students, even those who required the most attention. He enjoyed that challenge. What frustrated Mark was the system, the structured orthodoxies of education which Mark saw as the equivalent of a factory production line where students were to be shaped into predetermined, carefully measured units then moved along at a steady pace. What frustrated Mark was the dehumanization of it all, the constant effort to compress and standardize the students rather than to free them to appreciate their own individuality.

Mark described his feelings to a sympathetic colleague. "I care deeply about these students and want desperately to see them succeed," he said. "But here is the rub. I find myself encouraging them to succeed in a system with which I morally disagree. I don't want them to conform; I want them to resist and find voice. Yet, in order to do that, they have to understand the hierarchy that is oppressing them.

"I remember one time the principal told me that my altruistic tendencies were a liability in that I never saw the bad in students. I don't know if my outrage showed visibly, but my words came quickly: 'What's wrong with that?' He went on to tell me that I could not and should not 'mother' my students because that took the objectivity away and allowed students to get too close. In order to keep my job, I kept my mouth shut, but inside I was appalled that anyone could think that teaching was removed from love.

"Students need to have teachers who care about them, not just about their test scores, to understand that it's not wrong to be different. I listen to them but caution them as well without shutting them down. Most of all I don't want them to see me as the only authority in the room."

As the years passed, Mark had hoped that he could win over his colleagues. He wanted them to see that teaching was not mass production. The goal should be to help students to find their own individuality and the benefits of that. But he had little success in this effort and increasingly found himself marginalized by other faculty members. Most of them liked Mark and most admired his persistent pursuit of his own values, but few ever came around to believing that those values were the proper foundation of their own or the school's educational philosophy.

Mark is now contemplating resigning at the end of the current school year. His enthusiasm for teaching is undimmed, but he has lost hope of ever succeeding in constructing the educational environment he seeks. His father's death last fall has left an opening for him in the family business that would pay him far more than his current salary, and he must decide soon whether to change jobs.

What advice would you give him if he sought your counsel about these career decisions?

Discussion

According to Fried (2001), passion is a necessary quality of a teacher. But passionate convictions in one person often confront equally passionate but opposite convictions in others. Often one person's passion clashes with rules and procedures that seem to stifle or deflect it in another.

Mark's passion for teaching has served his students well. Most of their parents express gratitude for his efforts to encourage the individual strengths of their children. His impact on his students is as large as any teacher in the school.

Mark's problem is not passion, but patience—and tolerance. He wants everyone to be like him, and more important, to think like him. And since that is never likely to happen, his frustration is certain to endure.

There are never enough teachers like Mark, teachers who want to challenge prevailing orthodoxies to improve the quality of teaching and learning. He is a valuable part of his school community even if few others concur completely with his ideas. He forces them to think about what they do, to reflect on their own standards, to justify their own approaches. Everyone is more thoughtful and the community is stronger when teachers like Mark ask hard and constant questions.

We have all encountered teachers who did not want to go along with school policies because they thought they were stupid or too much work or they simply did not want to change the way they had always done things. Many of them cause problems for their colleagues and school administrators because they resist change.

Mark is the opposite of that. He is an agent of change, a provocateur who forces his colleagues to reflect constantly on the way they do their jobs. People like Mark make schools better.

Mark needs some help in understanding his value to his school. He needs to accept debate and disagreement as healthy ingredients in the recipe for effective schools. Just as he wants others in the community to listen to him, so must he learn to listen to them. Some of the love he tried to show his students might be expended with equal value on his colleagues. Life as a provocateur, no matter how valuable, is never easy. He needs to be professional and understanding while still working toward change and reform, to be more patient in his impatience (Freire, 2004).

If he can do that, and if he can find satisfaction in understanding his role in the school and his value in performing that role, and if he can continue to enjoy the rewards of effectiveness in his work with the students in his own classes, then Mark should be able to compartmentalize and channel his frustration with the "system" in ways that allow him to stay on as a teacher and to love the work that he does. It would be a tragedy if he chose to do otherwise.

WHAT ABOUT THE BOYS?

One of the things that attracted Tom to Midland High was the opportunity to implement some of the programs he had studied while doing his graduate work in Chicago. Tom had been a teacher for more than a decade and then a guidance counselor for six years after that. He decided to take time to get a graduate degree because he hoped he would then be able to head a guidance program at a large high school and have a direct impact on student lives. Midland High seemed a perfect fit for Tom's goals.

But Tom quickly came to realize that the practical implementation of his ideas would not be simple. Every school has its own culture, and changing a culture can be a daunting task. Midland was a community in transition. Formerly a town dominated by steel mills, it was rapidly becoming a residential and increasingly wealthy suburb. The steel mills were all closed now, and many of the people who once worked there remained in Midland but struggled to earn a living. At the same time, the once rural areas of the town were being developed into comfortable neighborhoods of large and expensive homes.

Nowhere was the transition more acutely felt than at the high school. Tom's initial impressions were that it was more like two high schools that share the same building. There was the more traditional Midland High that was little more than a rite of passage for young men on their way to work in the steel mills and the young women who would become their wives. The steel mills were gone but the young men and women, children of the former steelworkers, were still there.

The newer Midland High was composed of the children of those who had moved into the community over the past two decades. Their families were wealthier and had much higher aspirations for their children. To them, Midland was a preparatory school for college and a life in the upper middle class.

All of this posed many challenges for the guidance department that Tom had been hired to lead. As he assessed the situation in his first few weeks on the job, he came to the realization that the "tough boys" would have to be his highest priority. This was the name that some of the teachers at Midland had given to the group of male students who came from the more traditional side of the community. School held no special appeal or significance to them. They brought little energy or initiative to their coursework. They rarely engaged in extracurricular activities except football. And far too many of them never graduated.

In reviewing their records and talking to some of the teachers, Tom noticed that many of these tough boys seemed to enjoy technical courses and performed much more successfully in those than they did in the more traditional classes like English, history, and biology. Tom never felt that the tough boys were a lost cause. He believed instead that teaching strategies in the school had to evolve to reach out

(Continued)

(Continued)

to this group of students to make school more appealing to them and more attuned to their learning styles. It was his goal to convince the faculty of the need to do that.

But this is where Tom ran into problems. There were a few teachers who shared his view and his optimism about the possibility of making Midland High a more hospitable place for this group of male students. Tom engaged these teachers in discussion of an initiative that would have two components. First, it would try to bring to traditional academic courses more opportunities for students to do hands-on work and a focus on the practical applications of what they were learning. Second, Tom and the guidance department would work with the faculty to provide timely, focused support in core curricula along with study and organizational skills to give struggling students a better chance to succeed.

Tom and the small group of sympathetic teachers drafted a proposal for accomplishing these two objectives. But when they began to circulate it, they quickly encountered much more opposition than Tom had imagined. There seemed to be two groups in the faculty who were unsupportive. One was a group of mostly young teachers who had come to the school in the last few years and who saw it as a place where high academic standards should prevail to ensure that the best students in the community would have every opportunity for admission to the top universities in the country and for successful careers and lives. Some of those teachers and others aspired to live in the newly developed parts of Midland. They had little sense of Midland's former identity as a steel town and little interest in shifting their teaching focus from the best students with the highest aspirations to the lower achieving students with lower aspirations. To them, curriculum decisions were a zero-sum game. Time and effort spent on struggling students was time not spent on the most engaged students.

Opposition also came from another group of teachers, many of whom had been at the school for decades, who thought Tom's initiative was hopeless. They did not believe there was any way to engage the tough boys. They had tried things like this before. Having seen generations of these boys pass through their school, they had little hope that any program at Midland High could overcome the lack of intellectual and emotional support they received at home. They also believed that these were tough boys because they came from a community culture that placed a very high value on toughness and a very low value on intellectual curiosity or school learning. This group of teachers thought the tough boys were largely unreachable. It was a waste of time and effort to try to penetrate their resistance to school. The dropout rate among the tough boys was a fact of life and, in their view, simply normal. In any class, there would be certain number of dropouts and that was just the way of the world or at least the way of life in Midland.

Tom decided he could hold off on his initiative until he had been at the school a while longer, not wanting to begin his tenure there in a big battle with key elements of the faculty. But the more he analyzed the situation, the more convinced he was that something had to be done to reach out to the tough boys.

Tom spent some time observing these boys in tech classes and outside of school. He saw that they actually had plenty of academic and organizational skills. What they seemed to lack was a sense of meaning and connection with schooling. School offered them few intellectual or social incentives, so they chose not to have much to do with what went on there. Tom became more convinced that structures and processes at Midland High needed to be changed in order to provide meaningful learning for these students. He felt that the school had been sacrificing this particular group of students for its own reputation in this era of heightened accountability and in a community where post-secondary aspirations were growing. To him, it was not simply bad educational policy to treat the tough boys as they had been treated, it was unethical.

By the end of his first year at Midland, Tom realized that he could wait no longer. If he did not act to improve the opportunities for the tough boys, he would be violating his own educational philosophy and what he believed to be his highest obligation as an educator.

Do you agree with Tom's assessment of the situation? How would you proceed were you in his place?

Discussion

Before taking further action, Tom has to think carefully about his short- and long-term goals. His long-term goal appears to be a significant change in school culture. He wants the school to move beyond its tolerance for persistently failing to engage the tough boys. Since that tolerance is so deeply embedded in the existing school culture—it has been like that for years—and since the changes taking place in the demographics of Midland continue to shift the focus of attention away from struggling students and toward those with higher aspirations, Tom has his work cut out for him. If he expects a quick turnaround in school culture, he is likely to be disappointed.

So a more prudent approach might be to seek ways to demonstrate the validity of his views by undertaking a kind of demonstration project. He might, for example, recruit a few teachers to work with him in developing a program that combines reading instruction and skill development with more hands-on, practical learning opportunities. Then Tom and these teachers might implement this program with some of the tough boys who are enrolled in their courses. And to be able later to demonstrate their results to the entire school community, they would want to follow standard research practices by interviewing or pretesting the boys in the program, monitoring their progress at milestones through the year, and then reinterviewing or retesting them at the end of the year. To create an approximation of an experimental design, they might employ the same testing and interviewing methods with another group of the boys in other classes without any special program aimed at them.

If this approach demonstrates that progress can be made in more fully engaging the tough boys in the learning process and in the life of the school, Tom and his colleagues will be able to use their findings to encourage broader support among the faculty and wider implementation of the program they have developed.

Tom may view the failure to reach out proactively to the tough boys as the heart of the ethical issue and that it violates his fundamental and dearly held principles. But he should be cautious about posing his proposals for change in any form that resembles an ethical ultimatum. Some of those he seeks to convince may not regard this as an ethical issue at all but rather as a technical question of effective and efficient pedagogy.

Others may see ethical principles at stake here but feel that Tom is focused on the wrong principle. To them, the right approach might be utilitarian—the greatest good for the greatest number, in which case, resources should be focused on the students most likely to benefit from them and not on students who, by their own choice, have declined to take advantage of the opportunities available at Midland High.

Resistance to change in a school can come from several different sources. It may come from the clash of educational philosophies, it may come from a deeply embedded school culture, or it may come from simple inertia. Change agents must always begin by assessing the challenges they face and the sources of the resistance they must overcome (Evans, 1996; Fullan, 2004).

Once they have done that, then they must begin to develop strategies for convincing other members of their school communities that change is desirable and necessary. In the cases discussed here, we see one other task confronting change agents: To convince reluctant members of the community that change is possible.

Institutions always profit from people who ask tough and responsible questions about their operations. Schools do especially, and they ought to welcome those questions and listen and respond to the people who raise them. But resistance to change and reluctance to change are normal, and if the proponents of change hope to have an impact, they must approach their task with a clear recognition of its difficulty and with a willingness to tolerate those who do not share their enthusiasms. Change is an educational process, and when philosophies or values clash in a school, it is important to grasp the opportunity for those on one side to engage in constructive dialogue with those on the other. Schools that encourage such conversations cannot help but benefit from the outcomes they yield.

For Reflection and Conversation

Because this chapter deals with the clash of philosophies, we conclude it by suggesting some readings to expand your thinking in the ways the teachers featured in this chapter have done. Rather than offer cases here for your consideration, we provide a resource list to prompt your thinking about various educational philosophies and pedagogies. As you can imagine, one's philosophy of education, of teaching and learning, and of schooling develops from experiences but also from reading, conversation, and reflection. We encourage you to delve into some of these contemporary writers on ways to think about the role of schooling in the lives of children and young adults and also to revisit some of the writers who resonated with you while you were a student, particularly, a student of pedagogy. Rather than see the ethics of justice, care, or critique as mutually exclusive, we urge you to think of ways each can inform your thinking and imbue your actions with depth and openness of thought. We hope these will prove beneficial to you and to your fellow teachers as you investigate ways that schools can help light the path to social justice and equality.

Resources for Expanding Your Perspective

Ayers, W. (2004). *Teaching toward freedom: Moral commitment and ethical action in the classroom.* Boston: Beacon Press.

Briscoe, F., Arriaza, G., & Henze, R. C. (2009). *The power of talk: How words change our lives.* Thousand Oaks, CA: Corwin.

Freire, P. (2004). *Pedagogy of the oppressed.* New York: Continuum.

Goodlad, J. I., Soder, R., & Sirotnik, K. A., Eds. (1990). *The moral dimensions of teaching.* San Francisco: Jossey-Bass.

Green, M. (2000). *Releasing the imagination: Essays on education, the arts, and social change.* San Francisco: Jossey-Bass.

hooks, b. (1994). *Teaching to transgress: Education as the practice of freedom.* London: Routledge.

Katz, M. S., Noddings, N., & Strike, K. A., Eds. (1999). *Justice and caring: The search for common ground in education.* New York: Teachers College Press.

Noddings, N. (2003). *Caring: A feminine approach to ethics and moral education* (2nd ed.). Berkeley: University of California Press.

Palmer, P. (2007). *The courage to teach: Exploring the inner landscape of a teacher's life.* New York: John Wiley & Sons.

Starratt, R. (2005). *Ethical leadership.* San Francisco: Jossey-Bass.

8

Clashing Codes

Professional Communities of Teachers

Teachers, guidance counselors, coaches, librarians, and administrators are education professionals. As such, they bear responsibilities not simply to their schools and the colleagues with whom they work every day but also to the standards and values established by their professions (Shapiro & Stepkovich, 2005). For many school employees, primary contact with others who hold jobs like theirs in other schools comes through their memberships in professional associations.

Those associations establish standards, accredit preparation programs, certify individual training, and conduct opportunities for continuing education, among other roles. Many associations publish newsletters and reports that help their members stay informed about changes in policy and law that may affect their performance in the schools that employ them.

Within their own schools, some of these professionals have specific roles and responsibilities that permit or require them to become resources for others in the school. Guidance counselors, for example, are expected to be knowledgeable about the current state of the law with regard to such things as reporting family violence incidents. Teachers may turn to guidance counselors for advice on how to deal with such situations when students describe them.

There are times when the standards of an employee's profession may come into conflict with the needs or wishes of others with whom he or she works. It is not uncommon, for example, for a well-intentioned teacher to want to do something that violates the standards that other school employees are obligated to uphold. We will see such a conflict between a teacher and school librarian in the first case below. Such conflicts can raise ethical dilemmas because they force school employees to choose between two attractive alternatives. The question that often arises is, how far should an employee go in asserting and protecting professional standards when those may have a negative impact, at least in the short term, on classroom instruction.

Most public school teachers are also members of labor unions. These, too, are professional associations, established for the purpose of protecting the interests of their members. Teachers may also encounter conflicts between their responsibilities to their students, on the one hand, and their obligation to support the other members and leaders of their union on the other. This conflict can become especially aggravated when local unions are engaged in difficult negotiations with community school boards. Not uncommonly in those instances, unions decide on tactics that constrain their members' in-school activities—rarely a comfortable situation for a dedicated teacher.

The ethical tension here is clear: How does one do the right thing when trying to balance professional obligations and responsibilities with the needs of students and schools? The cases that follow suggest some of the dimensions of that challenge and offer some guidance for dealing with them.

THE COPYRIGHT POLICE

Ann Rowell is a teacher at Lower Valley Elementary School. She has long been admired by administrators for her ability to accomplish her goals in a school that is perpetually short of resources. "She is creative in finding ways to make do," one of her principals wrote in an assessment of her.

Recently Ann sent a fifth-grade student named Jeff to the school library with a note giving him permission to use the photocopier there. The new library media specialist, Arthur Lane, led Jeff to the copier, turned it on, and then went back to his own work. He noted, however, that Jeff was making multiple copies of dozens of pages from a workbook. A similar pattern ensued for each of the next several weeks: Jeff would arrive with a note from Ann Rowell and copy extensively from the workbook.

Arthur decided it was his responsibility to speak to Ann about this, so he approached her one day after the students had left. He had a copy of the workbook and directed Ann's attention to the copyright notice on the second page that indicated workbooks were to be for the use of a single student only and should not be reproduced in any way other than that indicated by the publisher.

Ann laughed at this. "Welcome to the real world, Arthur," she said. "I wish we could buy a new workbook for each student, but we have no budget for that. We haven't been able to buy new workbooks for three years. So we have no choice but to copy pages from the old ones and let students use the copies."

"But, Ann, that's a violation of the copyright laws that goes way beyond any notion of fair use," Arthur responded.

"Considering the price of the textbook, companies should give away the workbooks that go with it," Ann said. "Besides, these are old workbooks. We probably couldn't buy more if we wanted to."

"That doesn't matter," said Arthur. "The copyright laws apply even to materials that are old or out of print. A company can't sell the new editions if teachers keep copying the old ones. That's another reason we have copyright laws."

"Well, turn me in to the cops if you want, Arthur. But understand that you'll just be hurting our students. If I don't copy pages from these old workbooks, they won't have anything to work on because we're sure not going to be able to afford new ones." Ann smiled knowingly and turned to pack up her papers before heading home.

Arthur is uncertain how to proceed. He appreciates Ann's dilemma, but he also feels that schools need to teach ethical and appropriate use of published materials to students and that means observing copyright regulations. He also worries, now that he knows about it, that he is complicit in the violation if he does not try to stop Ann from further unauthorized copying.

What should Arthur do now?

Discussion

Arthur's obligations here are clear. One of his primary responsibilities within the school is to maintain professional standards and to uphold the law. He is trained to do that, and he was hired because of that training. However admirable her intentions, Ann's actions are wrong. If Arthur simply looks the other way, then he, too, has contributed to a violation of the law. He would then have failed in meeting his professional obligations. So there is no question that Arthur's primary duty is to uphold the copyright laws (Simpson, 2005).

Having thought about this and assured himself of his obligations, perhaps the next step for Arthur is to have another conversation with Ann. In this, he should be clear that he cannot permit further copying from the old workbooks. He might suggest to Ann that she communicate with the publisher of the workbooks to seek permission to make copies from out-of-print editions. But if Ann persists in attempting the unauthorized copying or having her students do it, Arthur will have no choice but to report the violation to his supervisor.

But what if Ann agrees to desist from further unauthorized copying? Is that the end of it? Or does Arthur also have an obligation to report the past violations of the copyright laws and, if so, to whom? In answering this question, Arthur might find it useful to consider the rule of publicity. Would he be comfortable in not reporting the past violations if it were widely known that he knew about them and did not report them? The answer, in all probability, is no. That suggests that the proper ethical course for Arthur is to report, at least to his supervisor, that there has been a pattern of violation of copyright laws in the school library.

No doubt, Arthur will find this difficult. He admires Ann and her dedication to her students despite a constant shortfall in resources. He wishes her no harm. But decisions of this sort—where complicated ethical questions are at the center—need to be resolved in a broad rather than a narrow context. Arthur should be as vigilant in supporting the copyright laws with the teacher he admires as he would with a teacher he dislikes. The issue here is not his feelings about the particular culprit, but his responsibility to uphold the law and maintain professional standards. The legal use of materials is part of a school librarian's education and interpreting the ever-changing laws in a digital age is a frequent topic for library conferences, articles, and workshops. Teaching the ethical and appropriate use of information is a crucial task for a library media specialist in a school (American Library Association/American Association of School Libraries, 2001).

It is not Arthur's role to determine how the school will deal with Ann, but he has an obligation to the school and to the standards of his profession to prevent this violation from passing without notice or response.

WHO OWNS THE POWERPOINT?

Dan is a high school history teacher, and his department has just revised its curriculum. As part of the revision, Dan will be teaching a course in the fall on the American Revolution, a topic that interests him but about which he has never before offered a course. So Dan is spending much of the summer preparing that course.

While searching the Internet for information one day, Dan comes across a wonderful PowerPoint presentation on the Constitutional Convention. He downloads it from the Internet and includes it in the materials he is preparing on that topic. During the fall, when his class reaches the unit on the convention, he uses the PowerPoint as a learning tool. At the end of the unit, he distributes the PowerPoint to his students electronically to help them study for the final exam.

A problem arises subsequently, however, when one of his students shows the materials from this class to his older sister who is a college student. The PowerPoint looks very familiar to her; in fact, it is exactly the same PowerPoint that her professor used in a history class she had taken the previous year. She searches for it online, finds it quickly, and shows her brother that the PowerPoint used in his high school history class was created by her college professor and "stolen" by Dan, his high school teacher.

The older sister mentions this to their father, who then calls the high school principal to report the theft of intellectual property. The principal, wanting to get the facts before making a determination about this, meets with Dan to discuss the matter. Dan tells them the truth—that he found the PowerPoint online and saw no problem using it in his class because any of his students could also have found it online on their own. To Dan, this meant simply that the creator of the PowerPoint had no intention to protect his intellectual property, that by placing it online, he was essentially giving it away for free to anyone who found it.

The principal appreciates Dan's candor but realizes there may be a policy issue here. How should teachers in the school deal with information which they acquire online and wish to use in class? What obligations, if any, do they have to the creators of that information?

Discussion

The concept of intellectual property has been evolving in the digital age. It is no longer as clear as it once was who "owns" information that is readily available online (Committee on Intellectual Property Rights and the Emerging Information Infrastructure, 2000). But one of the obligations of any school is to sensitize its employees and its students to the concept of intellectual property and the importance, at a minimum, of crediting the creators of original work for their contributions.

In this case, Dan clearly had an obligation to indicate to his students that the PowerPoint in question was not created by him and to identify its creator. Any teacher has a professional obligation to indicate to students the sources of information used in a class, especially information prepared in a specific format, for example, a text, a graphic, or slide presentation. Such crediting is central to the notion of good scholarship, but it is also important not to deceive students by taking credit for work that the teacher did not originate.

Dan might well go further here by contacting the professor who created the PowerPoint presentation and seeking her permission to use it in his own class. If such permission is granted explicitly, then no one can accuse Dan of unauthorized use of another person's intellectual property. Or, if such permission is not granted, Dan will know that he should not use the PowerPoint that he found online and then must find some other way to present information to his students.

The general rule is when in doubt, ask.

A COACH'S DILEMMA

Marty Bowen had waited 15 years to get a head-coaching job. After all those autumns of practices and games, of working under coaches from whom he learned and others for whom he had little respect, he can now run his own show. The team at Mid-County High School needed a lot of work, but it was just the kind of challenge that Marty relished. The team had had two consecutive losing seasons, but with a nucleus of experienced players and an apparent desire for improvement, the prospects for this season were much brighter.

But Marty also knew that the key to a successful season was going to be hard work. If the team practiced long and hard, it could overcome the losing habits and attitudes of previous seasons. One thing that worried Marty, however, was the new rules established by the state principals' association last spring. These limited the practice times of all high school athletic teams to no more than two hours a day, five days a week. As a member of the state coaches' association, Marty and all of the other coaches in his league were obligated to abide by the decisions of the principals' association.

After the first month of the season, Marty felt that his team was making progress. It had won two games and lost two, Marty felt that his players were on the verge of a real breakthrough. He only wished there was more time to work on the fundamentals and game strategies that might ensure a winning season the rest of the way.

One day after practice, the co-captains indicated to Marty that they intended to hold team practices on Saturday and Sunday mornings for the rest of the season without any of the coaches present. They would hold the practices at a field behind the barn on the farm of one of the players. No school property or school employees would be involved. It would not be any different, the co-captains said, than a pick-up game among friends—nothing that would violate any rules. And they knew from conversations they had had with other players at a football camp the previous summer that such weekend practices were common among the teams against which they competed.

Marty congratulated them for their initiative. He was pleased his players seemed to be developing a winning attitude and a commitment to match. When Marty described all this to his wife that night, she seemed distressed. "Don't you think this violates the spirit and the purposes of the principals' association ruling," she asked, "even if it doesn't do so in a technical sense?" Marty thought for a minute and then responded, "I don't agree. All rules are technical—any coach knows that. And we are technically within the rules. There won't be any coaches at these practices, and they won't be on school property. Besides, I know for a fact that many of the other schools in our league have weekend practices run by the team captains just like this. Everyone else does it. If we don't do this, the other teams will have a significant competitive advantage over us. And that's just not fair."

Do you agree with Marty about this?

Discussion

Marty is a member of a professional association that exists, among other purposes, to establish standards for its members. One of the obligations of such membership is to abide by, defend, and promote those standards. But in this case, Marty has acquiesced to behavior that challenges the standards his association seeks to maintain. He justifies that acquiescence in two ways.

First, he says that he will be technically in compliance with the standards and that it is not wrong if he knowingly allows members of his team to act in ways that threaten those standards. This is a common ethical dilemma: Is technical compliance enough? That is, is it sufficient to observe the minimum requirements of rules or laws or standards while permitting or participating in actions which, while not technically prohibited, undermine their purposes?

We suggest a couple of ways Marty could better answer this question. For example, he might ask himself whether he could defend his acquiescence in the weekend practices if their existence were publicized. If a sports reporter for the local paper were to call him and ask him about those practices, would Marty be comfortable justifying them? This is the application of the rule of publicity: Would an action or decision be acceptable if everyone knew about it?

Another good way to fortify the integrity of his actions here would be for Marty to consult with senior administrators and his peers at Mid-County High School. Do they agree with his assessment of the propriety of the weekend practices? Do those practices comport with the values and ethical standards of the school? Consultation, as we have noted often, is a way to collectivize a decision and solidify its ethical foundation.

At a minimum, because he has been informed by the captains of their plans and he has not told them to stop, Marty is complicit in the decision to hold weekend practices. This raises important considerations for the school system. Could the "practices" be considered a school activity even without the direct supervision of school employ-ees? What if one of the players is hurt during the weekend practices? Will there be proper and immediate medical attention? Might the other players avoid or delay calling for medical help to prevent detec-tion of these practices? What are the liability concerns for the school system if a student suffers harm in this activity?

As a school employee—and as a coach whose concern for the wel-fare of his student athletes should be his paramount concern Marty has to ask himself hard questions about the actions his captains are proposing. His responses should reflect the players' best interests and those of the school system that employs him. Any school employee who puts students at risk or his school system in jeopardy without consulting broadly before doing so is not acting ethically.

A second way in which Marty justifies his attitude about these weekend practices is by saying, "Everybody does it." But "everybody does it" is not an ethical principle; in fact, in most usages it is an excuse for violating ethical principles. If something is wrong, the fact that everybody does it does not make it right.

All the coaches may be condoning, perhaps even encouraging, these weekend practices, but Marty doubts whether they would be per-mitted under the rules established by the principals' association. The proper course of action for Marty is to seek an interpretation from the principals' association. If the association indicates that such practices do not violate its rules, then he can feel confident in permitting his co-captains to conduct them. If, on the other hand, the principals' associa-tion indicates that such weekend practices do violate the rules, then Marty's responsibilities are clear. He should notify the team members that they are not allowed to practice; furthermore, he could request that all the other coaches comply with this clarification of the rules as well.

WORKING TO RULE

In her 26 years as an elementary school special education teacher, Darlene Taggart had often been grateful for the efforts of the WEA, the statewide teach-ers union. Most public school teachers in the state are dues-paying members, and the local chapters of the union represented teachers in all of their contract nego-tiations with local school boards. In Darlene's town, the union had fought hard for wage and benefit increases that had given her sufficient financial security to continue in a career that she loved.

She loved her work because of the opportunities it afforded her to have a positive effect on the lives of her students. One student she had been working with since he was kindergarten was David, a boy with a difficult home life. Darlene had encouraged David to visit in her classroom for the hour or so after school while she prepared for the following day's work. Last year, he stayed almost every day. She had an opportunity to oversee his homework and to have conversations with him that she felt filled an important void in his life. In many ways, Darlene had taken on parenting responsibilities for David which made her feel good because she thought David had great potential and desperately needed adult support.

But Darlene faced a dilemma. Contract negotiations with the school board had stalled at the end of the previous year. As the current school year began, the teachers had no contract and the continuing lack of progress in the negotiations had led the local chapter of the union to decide that it was time for teachers to "work to rule." All teachers would do only the minimum required by their last contract. They would follow the contract and arrive at school when they were supposed to and leave immediately at the end of the time they were required to remain after school. They would take on no work or responsibilities beyond those of preparing and teaching classes. Working to rule was a common strategy in stalled contract negotiations in their state. It usually resulted in parental complaints about teachers no longer performing services upon which parents had come to rely and which everyone recognized were important to student learning. These complaints often pressured school boards to concede to the union's demands.

But for Darlene, this meant that she would no longer be able to spend the hours after school with David as she had for the past year. She was a loyal union member and she supported its tactics, but she did not feel in her heart that she could abandon David in this way. So she continued to stay after school each day, to do her work and to provide a safe and supportive place for David. She regretted that she could not fully embrace the union's tactic in its contract negotiations, but she felt she was doing the right thing.

Was she?

Discussion

When we join or participate in professional associations, we agree at least implicitly to adhere to their policies. But sometimes those policies may conflict in difficult ways with other professional obligations or personal values (Plante, 2004; Strike & Soltis, 1998). And we are forced to choose: Do we allow the professional association to determine our course or do we plot and pursue our own? This is rarely an easy choice.

By taking the action she has in this case, Darlene risks angering her colleagues perhaps with long-term consequences for her relationships with them. Union members who appear to undermine union tactics always risk being shunned or worse. Darlene confronts that risk. It should weigh heavily in her decision making here. Will her long-term effectiveness as a teacher be undermined by her short-term commitment to David?

On the other hand, Darlene may value her contributions to David's welfare more highly than the risks she faces in future relationships with her colleagues. In her view, the right thing in this situation is to do what is best for David even if that may cause her harm. Perhaps her colleagues will recognize the dilemma she faces and appreciate the choice she has made or perhaps not. That is a risk she may be willing to take.

Darlene might find some comfort, perhaps even some guidance, by consulting with teachers at her school with whom she has good relationships, seeking their advice on how to deal with this dilemma. They might not agree with the choices she wishes to make, but at least they will have a clearer sense of the dilemma she faces and realize that she is not simply disregarding the union.

Darlene might also find that there is a way to balance her loyalties here. Perhaps if she could find some appropriate place to go after school where she could spend time with David, she might satisfy the union's work to rule tactic. For example, she could spend some time at the local library or YMCA with David. A conversation with leaders of the local chapter of the union might help guide her through her dilemma; and, again, this might enhance their appreciation for her conscientious efforts to balance her support for the union with her commitment to the student.

Just as teachers have to balance maintaining relationships with colleagues with questioning and critique of their peers, so must they weigh their various commitments between professional organizations and children. Rather than seeing these "right versus right" dilemmas as insoluble conundrums, through consultation and analysis they may discover a third way (Kidder, 2003). Such a solution softens hard choices by suggesting a compromise approach, a win-win for everyone.

For Reflection and Conversation

The following are cases similar to the ones presented in this chapter. How would you analyze the individual's obligations, and what might be appropriate next steps for the teachers or other educators to take?

1. The guidance program in John's school provides services to all students starting in kindergarten. He and the other classroom teachers expect their "comprehensive" guidance program to reflect the policies and practices of the social curriculum that has been collectively developed, agreed upon, and implemented by all professionals in the school.

The guidance counselor at his school holds regular guidance classes as part of the school's social curriculum. She also promotes various sessions she offers to small groups of students each year on such topics as changing families, divorce, and children dealing with loss. Parents have to request that their children participate in any of these groups.

Some of the teachers, including John, have come to believe that the guidance counselor too often encourages students to feel and express suffering far beyond what they actually feel, to "let out their hidden feelings" even when such feelings may not really exist. By so doing, the teachers believe, the guidance counselor gives inappropriate support to students when they behave irresponsibly by not completing assignments or "acting out" in their relationships with other students. John believes that these kinds of behaviors have gotten worse since the guidance counselor came to work at his school.

The guidance counselor defends her work by arguing that her professional responsibility is to look out for the needs of the children with whom she works, to help them recognize and address the stresses in their lives, and to develop strategies for dealing with them. She does not believe that teachers have the same priorities but thinks that too often they simply want students to behave compliantly in class. As a professional, she argues, it would be wrong for her to change her approach to her work just to make life easier for teachers. Is she right?

2. Mary became a teacher in midlife. Before that, she attended divinity school and was the pastor of a local church. When the church was forced to close for financial reasons, she decided to pursue a new career as a teacher.

Although Mary's career changed, her religious fervor did not. She still feels obligated, as she says, to "live her life in service to God." In so doing, she often takes a few minutes during the school day, often while her students are working on an in-class assignment, to sit at her desk, bow her head, and pray. She does not ask the students to do this, nor even indicate orally to them that she is taking time to pray.

When one of the students told his parents about Mary's "prayer times," the parents were upset that this seemed to violate the constitutional separation of church and state and the interpretations of the federal courts that prohibit prayer in schools. They addressed their concerns to the principal in Mary's school who, in turn, asked Mary to stop visibly praying in class during school hours. Mary declined to do so, saying that she has not engaged students in these activities and thus has not violated the proscriptions against prayer in schools, but that her faith is strong and requires that she pray regularly as she makes decisions during the day.

How should the principal respond?

3. Ben is very active in national- and state-level teaching organizations. He is widely regarded as one of the leaders in advocating for innovative approaches to teaching and learning in its schools. A year ago, he became editor of a journal that

publishes articles about educational issues in the state. It is a scholarly journal, and all submissions are blind-reviewed by referees before a decision is made on whether to publish. As editor, Ben chooses the referees.

Recently a manuscript was submitted that reported on a study done by its authors. They found that a program for under-achieving middle schoolers was not accomplishing its objectives and was probably not worth the funds that the state education commissioner had committed to it. This was a program that Ben had worked hard to initiate. In selecting referees for this article, Ben purposely chose two people—one an employee of the state commissioner's staff, the other a professor at the state university—who had worked on the development of the program. Both recommended against publication of the manuscript.

By word of mouth, the authors of the manuscript learned the names of the referees. They felt that Ben's choices had stacked the odds against them. By choosing referees whom he believed to be supportive of the program the authors were criticizing, Ben had guaranteed that their manuscript would not be published. The authors accused Ben of a conflict of interest and of violating professional standards. Ben disagreed, responding that it was good and common practice to assign referees whom an editor knew were experts on the subject of a manuscript and likely to examine it critically.

Did Ben act properly?

4. Alice is a high school science teacher who specializes in biology. Most of her classes are for juniors and seniors in the introductory or advanced biology curriculum. But like all the science teachers, she also teaches one section each year of general science, primarily for freshmen. Since each of the teachers comes at this from different specializations, her department allows each teacher to select his or her own text and to emphasize the science discipline in which each is most knowledgeable. So some of the classes lean toward biology, others toward chemistry or physics.

One day at a department meeting, Alice notices that one of her colleagues is carrying a general science text that was published almost 15 years earlier. She had once used the book herself, earlier in her career, but realizes that much of what it contains is now out of date and some of it—because of new scientific advances—is simply wrong. She mentions this to her colleague but gets an angry response. "Remember," he says, "it's our policy to let teachers use whatever book we choose. I'm familiar with this book. I like it, and I can compensate in class for whatever problems there may be with it."

Alice is skeptical. Her colleague has a reputation for laziness, for not keeping up with his scientific field, and for being unwilling to try new teaching approaches. She fears that there are things in the book that he may not realize are wrong and that students may be learning them without any correction from him. She recognizes that academic freedom is an important value among teachers but so, too, is pursuit of the truth. She wonders what, if anything, she should do about this.

Where do her professional obligations lie?

PART IV

Acting Ethically: Teachers and Supervisors

States are not moral agents; people are and can impose moral standards on powerful institutions.

—Noam Chomsky

9

Power and Authority

Teachers and Their Principals

P otential pitfalls inhabit every work relationship where one person supervises—essentially has power over—another. The person in power might ask subordinates to do something that they think is inappropriate, wrong, or unethical. A subordinate may observe behavior on the part of the person in power which he or she believes to be wrong or unethical. Or subordinates may act in ways that undermine the legitimate authority and effective leadership of the person in power (Blase & Blase, 2002).

> Bureaucratic organizations rely on a hierarchy of authority for coordination and control, whereas professional organizations rely on trust in the expertise of the professionals to exercise discretion in responding to the needs of clients. Schools are a unique combination of bureaucratic and professional organizations. . . . Trust depends, in part, on what one expects of another on the basis of formal roles and informal norms. The reality of life in organizations is that individuals are invested with varying degrees of power and authority. (Tschannen-Moran, 2004, p. 36)

Even though schools claim to have flatter organizations and are working toward shared leadership, the supervisory hierarchy remains. In schools, the most common relationship of this sort is between principals and teachers. A principal has power and authority that he or she may not even realize or understand.

While both teachers and principals may have the same objective—to provide optimum conditions for student learning—they may have very different views on how best to accomplish this. And because they work together in a complex environment, there are constant opportunities for misunderstandings, disagreements, and disputes. Forging and maintaining good working relations between those who hold leadership positions and those who perform the essential work of the school is an ongoing challenge in any school (Donaldson, 2006). That challenge is never more acute than when ethical issues threaten the relationship between principal and teacher.

When ethical disagreements or dilemmas arise, it is important that they be recognized as soon as possible and that all parties participate in resolving them. Well-managed schools develop protocols and procedures for dealing with ethical issues, and in such schools, open discussion is welcomed and encouraged. Those in leadership positions understand the burden falls on them—not to set the ethical standards since this is rarely done effectively from the top down—but to encourage the kind of open discussion and critique that ensures that all school employees will see themselves as stakeholders in the development and protection of high ethical standards (Pellicer, 2003; Sockett, 1990).

But no school can ever fully insulate itself from the ethical disagreements and dilemmas that are inevitable in the relationships among the school's employees and between them and the students and families they serve. The following cases illustrate the kinds of issues that often occur in relationships between principals and teachers. In reading them, think not only about immediate resolutions to the specific issues they raise but how schools might establish procedures for avoiding the kinds of problems these cases highlight as well as how schools could develop reliable and effective dispute-resolution mechanisms to resolve them when they occur.

TAKING MATTERS INTO HER OWN HANDS

Timmy, a second grader, has had some problems with other children outside school. Timmy and three other boys from the class were playing together after school, and two of the boys told their parents that Timmy touched them inappropriately. One of the parents then talked to Timmy's parents about this. Timmy's parents indicated that they appreciated the alert and that they would deal with it. No one brought this incident to the attention of any teacher or school administrator.

A few weeks later on a blustery day, Jenna, their teacher, returned from patrolling the halls for indoor recess duty to two anxious boys who told her that Timmy "had done stuff that we're not supposed to do." Jenna sent the two boys to the principal's office where Marlene, the principal, spoke with them. She subsequently spoke with Timmy as well. Since Jenna knew all the parents involved, she asked Marlene if she should call the parents. Marlene said that it was her responsibility and that she would call them.

As Jenna thought about this over the course of the day, she wondered if she should call social services. She remembered a teachers' conference from a year ago where teachers were advised always to alert professionals when incidents of potential abuse occurred, even if children were the perpetrators. When Jenna talked to Marlene later in the afternoon, she asked her about reporting the incident to social services. Marlene told Jenna to "calm down." She had called Timmy's mother and told her that if anything like this happened again, she would have to report it. Jenna said she thought the law required that this be reported to social services, but Marlene just shook her head and said, "It's pretty ambiguous what needs to be reported, especially when it's kids playing with kids. If you tell the story to 10 different lawyers, you'll get 10 different responses about what we should do."

Jenna wanted to do the right thing and felt she had an ethical obligation to call social services, despite Marlene's caution. So she did. The next day, Timmy's mother angrily accosted the principal in her office saying that Marlene had told her one thing then done another. Marlene did not know that Jenna had called social services and said so to Timmy's mother. She apologized for Jenna's actions.

Marlene was angry that Jenna had gone behind her back on this. Later in the day, after she had cooled down, she spoke to Jenna and told her that she had no right to call social services, that such a call was a job for the school principal. "Teachers," she said, "are not trained in school law and shouldn't be running off to the authorities on their own whenever they feel like it. Now you've humiliated me with a parent, raised questions about my management of the school with social services, and, no doubt, generated a lot of unnecessary concern among other parents in Timmy's class. This was a controllable situation, but you blew it way out of proportion."

How would you assess the behavior of Jenna and Marlene in this situation?

Discussion

Ethical dilemmas often arise out of conflicts between desirable objectives. In this case, Jenna was anxious to protect her students from possible abuse. Marlene, on the other hand, wanted to protect the perpetrator from being stigmatized by what might have been an isolated incident; and she wanted to manage the situation conservatively so as not to alarm other parents unnecessarily. Jenna was right to be concerned about potential risk to her students, and she was right to wonder if she or the school were legally required to contact an outside agency like social services. She brought her concerns to the principal which was also the right course of action.

When the principal's response left Jenna unsatisfied, she took action on her own without telling Marlene what she intended to do. She could have handled this in other ways, all of them preferable to the approach she followed. For example, she might have told Marlene that she was not in agreement with her analysis of the situation and thought that both of them should seek the advice of someone especially knowledgeable about school law, perhaps the superintendent or the school system's attorney.

If Marlene declined to pursue this course, then Jenna should have indicated to her explicitly her intention to contact social services on her own. When a teacher and principal disagree in a situation like this, where students are potentially at risk, a teacher need not be prevented from acting in a student's best interests even when told by a principal not to do so. But when such disagreement occurs, the teacher should clearly describe the action she intends to take to the principal and her reasons for doing so. Secrecy and surprise are rarely good ways to do business in any setting.

Whether or not Jenna's call to social services was an appropriate response to this incident, making the call without telling Marlene that she intended to do so was inappropriate. Jenna's knowledge that Marlene had already told Timmy's mother that she would not act unless there was another similar incident underscores the difficulties that Jenna created by making the call without informing Marlene.

School leaders, such as Marlene, often have to make judgment calls in their responses to situations that occur regularly in their schools. Determining when the interactions among students, especially very young students, cross a line that require outside intervention is one of the most difficult kinds of judgments that school leaders are called upon to make. Since Marlene did not know about the incident that occurred outside of school prior to the one that occurred in school, to her knowledge this was a first offense and perhaps an isolated incident. In that case, it was not unreasonable for her to believe that consultation with the parents might prevent any repetition of the offending behavior.

But when Jenna approached her about this, her response was insufficient. Clearly, the teacher was troubled and believed that the law required consultation with an outside agency. Marlene dismissed this concern, not by citing from any text or guidance on school law, but only by indicating that her obligations were unclear. A much better response would have been for Marlene to suggest that she would consult with the appropriate authority, again perhaps the superintendent or school system attorney, to determine whether she was obligated to bring this incident to the attention of outside agencies. She dismissed the teacher's legitimate concern too lightly and too flippantly in this case, which may well have invited Jenna to believe that she was more concerned with the reputation of the school than with the best interests of its students.

We should also note that Timmy's mother bears some responsibility here. While it is easy to understand that no parents would find this a comfortable situation, especially if they become the target of a social services investigation, there have now been two situations in which Timmy has acted inappropriately. For parents, this should be a very bright red flag indicating that their child has a behavior problem that demands immediate attention before it creates even angrier reactions. Perhaps the appropriate response for Timmy's parents in this situation would have been to ask Marlene's advice on how best to deal with it and to speak directly to Jenna to consult with her as well.

This is a difficult situation and a troubling one for Timmy and his parents. But the ethical dilemma that it posed could have been much more effectively dealt with if there had been more open and direct communication between the teacher and principal. And broader consultation with knowledgeable people not directly involved in the incident could have guided them to a proper course of action.

MUTUAL PROTECTION

Jon is the foreign language department chair at Lakeview High School, and he is having difficulty with Beth, a new teacher in the department. Beth had left a 10-year career in international business and had taught for three years in another school district after gaining certification.

Almost from the day she arrived, Beth caused dissension in the department. She was very serious about her teaching and had strong opinions on pedagogy and curriculum which she was not hesitant to share. The principal at her former school had indicated in recommending her that she was very talented in the classroom but strong willed and opinionated in dealing with colleagues. The principal at Lakeview, in spite of the misgivings Jon expressed following the interviews, had hired her. Yet Jon had to concede that none of the other candidates for the job could teach two languages nor had Beth's proven teaching skills.

(Continued)

(Continued)

But Beth quickly became a wedge in the department. She did not like to follow the curriculum and give the common assessments. She seemed to disagree with everything Jon said or did, though she usually expressed those disagreements to other teachers when he was not present. She cultivated friendships with younger teachers and tried to get them to see things her way. Jon had learned that she was even sending e-mails to others accusing Jon of saying and doing things he had not said or done. Jon was desperate to determine a course of action.

The department perennially wrestled with how to deal with students who received different kinds of preparation in middle school. Beth said that at her previous school they just placed all of them in the second year of the language. This seemed impossible to Jon, and it inspired him to call the department head at the school where Beth previously worked, a man he did not know. He informed Jon that what Beth had said about placing all entering students from middle school in second-year language was not accurate. They then had a conversation about Beth in which the other department head indicated the frustrations he had experienced in dealing with her and "her pathological unwillingness to trust anyone in authority or a leadership position." He indicated his sympathy for Jon and his relief that he no longer had to deal with Beth.

Then he said, "I'm going to tell you some things off the record that will help you understand what you're dealing with." There was a moment of silence when it seemed to Jon that he was shuffling some papers. "This is from her personnel file here." He went on to read from a number of memos in which Beth had complained to the principal and, in some cases, to the school board about the alleged incompetence of her colleagues. He also read from several file memos dictated by the principal describing conversations in which Beth had been told to stop these communications because they were damaging to faculty morale. He also described to Jon a petition that Beth had circulated calling for the resignation of his predecessor as foreign language department chair. "That tells you what she's like," he said. "But keep this confidential since this is all from a personnel file."

Jon felt reassured. Since Beth would be evaluated for tenure in a few months, Jon decided he should act quickly to keep Beth from becoming a permanent affliction in the department. He arranged a meeting with Tom, the principal, to talk about Beth.

At the meeting, Jon explicitly detailed the problems Beth was causing in the department. Then he described the phone conversation with the department chair at Beth's former school and the particulars he had provided from her personnel file. He said he regretted violating a confidence, but he felt it was for a greater good.

The principal listened intently and took notes on the information Jon provided. Then he said, "Because you shared that confidential information with me, let me share some with you." Beth had written a confidential e-mail to the school system personnel director complaining about the principal in unflattering, even vicious, terms. The personnel director, a personal friend, immediately told the principal, alerting him, he said, to the "devil in his midst."

> The principal, obviously, could not confront Beth with this information since it was all supposed to be confidential. But he indicated to Jon that he would be gathering whatever information he could find in the months ahead to be able to make a strong case for denying her tenure when that decision was made in the spring. He asked Jon to be diligent in providing any negative information he could gather as well.
>
> How would you assess the actions of Jon, Beth, and Tom in this case?

Discussion

There's a great deal of ethical trespassing in this case. Beth is a troublemaking employee who seems willing to use any means necessary to undermine Jon's ability to lead the department. Though she may be a good teacher, she has shown herself to be an insufferable colleague. It is understandable that Jon and Tom wish they had not hired her.

But their behavior is indefensible as well. They have both leapt to the conclusion that the way to deal with the problems Beth has caused is by denying her tenure and forcing her out of the school. Perhaps, ultimately, that will be necessary. But there are reasonable steps they can pursue now to address the problems that Beth has caused and seek to cure them. At a minimum, they should sit down with Beth, specify the actions that have caused them unhappiness, and suggest remedies. They should also work with Beth to improve interactions within the foreign language department and to establish a timetable for reviewing their progress in accomplishing that. It would not be inappropriate to indicate to Beth that her contributions to good relations within the department will be a significant consideration in their decision about her tenure.

Jon and Tom are both guilty of ethical lapses in the way they have treated confidential information. In a phone conversation with the department chair at Beth's former school, Jon should have stopped him as soon as he realized he was reading from a confidential personnel file. It would have been prudent for him to say something like, "I think it best that you not read to me from a confidential file." Once he had the information from that file, however, he had a further obligation not to share it, even with Tom.

Similarly, Tom crossed the line when he shared confidential information with Jon. In both cases, the violations of confidentiality seemed to serve the ultimate purpose of finding a way to get rid of Beth. But the end rarely justifies the means, and it surely does not do so here. Jon and Tom should have been looking for short-term ways to alter Beth's behavior and improve her chances for remaining at the school, not simply for evidence to use against her. But no matter what their goal, violations of confidentiality in personnel matters were an improper way to proceed. Both actors should have recognized that and cautioned the other.

COACHING FROM THE PRINCIPAL'S OFFICE

Marlon Barker was probably the best athlete ever to come out of Overland High School. He was captain of three sports and all-state in basketball two years in a row. He went on to the state university where he set the all-time scoring record. He was drafted by the pros, but a knee injury prevented him from playing. So he began his career as a coach and physical education teacher back at Overland. Now, 15 years later, he has just become the principal. To many in the community, this is a happy development. People there remember Marlon as a great sports hero and as a wonderful emblem of quality for their school.

Among the teachers at Overland, however, there is a wide disparity of views about their principal. Some, particularly those who grew up in the community, are pleased that Marlon now leads the school and feel that the community will be more supportive of the school led by a local hero than it would be if a stranger were the principal.

Other teachers, however, see Marlon's appointment as yet another example of the overemphasis on athletics at Overland High, and they especially worry that their principal has very little interest in the academic program. One of them was at the state university when Marlon was a student there and told his colleagues that, as a star athlete, Marlon was rarely required to attend classes and skated through his entire academic program. "If he learned anything at all," the teacher told colleagues, "it was entirely accidental. He was all about basketball; he never gave a thought to his academic work."

Now some of these teachers have another reason for concern. Since his appointment as principal, Marlon has established a special academic "counseling" program for Overland athletes. They are allowed—in fact, most are required by their coaches—to attend so-called study sessions during the last school period of the day and on Saturday mornings. Initially, these teachers applauded Barker's initiative. But then they learned more about it. They discovered that instead of helping athletes improve their study skills and mastery of substantive material, the coaches and some of the more academically able students were doing homework assignments for certain students so they could be sure to pass their courses and stay eligible to compete. The teachers learned this from students who are not athletes. They think it is unfair that athletes are getting special treatment. They say, "The coaches are helping them cheat on their homework."

Alice was more troubled by this than most of the other teachers. She had been at the school for two decades. She had taught Marlon Barker when he was a student there. She never liked him very much and had been deeply disappointed when he came back to coach at the school and then became principal. She always despised the overemphasis on athletics at Overland High and to her Marlon Barker was a monument to that. Now, it seemed, this "counseling" program for athletes was the last straw.

In the teachers' lounge one day, Alice raised her concerns with two of her colleagues. She said, "We need to go to the superintendent about this, maybe even to the school board. Those of us who take our academic responsibilities seriously are in an environment that grows increasingly inhospitable. It gets worse and worse, and we have to do something about it."

But her colleagues, though supportive of her analysis, would not go along with her proposed response. One argued, "If we do what you suggest, Alice, things will only be worse. The superintendent hired Marlon Barker as the principal. He's invested in Barker and it would make him look bad if he had to criticize his appointee's primary initiative as principal. And the school board members are all community folks who still love the guy as a sports hero. Remember how enthusiastic they were when the superintendent proposed him as principal. You think they're going to side with us against him? Hah!"

Alice realizes that her colleagues have probably accurately assessed the political realities. But she still feels that something has to be done.

What advice would you give her?

Discussion

It is important for Alice to distinguish the broader contextual problem of Overland High's emphasis on athletics from the more focused concern she has with the counseling program Marlon Barker has established for athletes, which she believes to be little more than institutionalized cheating. Her concern about the emphasis on athletics is a matter of policy that she should pursue through normal policy-making channels, such as discussions at faculty meetings and other forums where the policies of the school are normally discussed and decided (Enomoto & Kramer, 2007).

But her concern about the counseling program is an ethical issue, not a policy question. She believes that it is wrong for coaches or anyone else to do a student's homework and then allow the student to submit it as his or her own work. It would be wrong if a single coach did this in a single instance for a single student. But the magnitude of the impropriety is vastly multiplied when the school—or, in this case, the principal—sponsors a program that encourages this kind of unethical activity. Alice is right to be concerned and right to believe that she should take action. But what action should she take?

When confronting perceived ethical violations, the first step is usually to have a discussion with the violator. In this case, that would suggest that Alice should meet with Barker to raise her concerns about the counseling program for athletes. If there are other teachers who share her concerns, she should try to get them to join her in this discussion with the principal. She should indicate that some students feel that athletes are getting special treatment in this program and that she and other teachers have come to believe that coaches or students are actually doing the homework that some of the athletes submit.

Perhaps this will encourage the principal to eliminate the program or to alter it so that it serves the legitimate purpose of improving the study skills and academic performance of the athletes. If, however, Marlon denies Alice's criticisms and refuses to change or eliminate the program, she will then be obligated to take her concerns elsewhere, perhaps to the superintendent or the school board.

Confronting the principal is the appropriate first step in addressing an ethical impropriety in the school. But if the goal is not accomplished there, it cannot be the last step (Chaleff, 2003). The political odds that Alice and her like-minded colleagues face may appear to be stacked against them. But that cannot be an excuse for acquiescence in an unethical activity in their school. They are obligated to exhaust all of their options to right the wrong they perceive. Perhaps they will not succeed, creating another problem for themselves. But they will have done the right thing only if they try.

We have noted how difficult it is to sacrifice relationships with colleagues to take an ethical stand. Teachers may be risking more than a relationship by standing up to a supervisor. Nevertheless, teachers must recognize their personal and professional obligation to ensure that schools attend to the values of fairness and honesty. It may involve questioning both colleagues and administrators, not to mention the community, when they feel the need to expose institutionalized inequities schools may have engaged in for a long time. Society has come a long way in righting some of the prejudices and privileges woven into our traditions. Teachers acting courageously have played an important role in that progress.

For Reflection and Conversation

Here are cases developed by teachers who are struggling with issues similar to the ones in this chapter. How would you analyze their situations and help them to sort out action steps?

❖ ❖ ❖

1. Last night at the school board meeting, I was stunned when the chair of the board asked the principal of my school to come forward and accept a framed certificate praising him for raising the math scores of the students in our school by a larger percentage than in any other elementary school in the state. In handing him the certificate, the board chair said this accomplishment was emblematic of the leadership he had shown since he became principal and of his creative approaches to learning. The principal then said a few words, thanking the board for its confidence in him and pledging that he would continue to pursue every creative opportunity to improve the quality of his school and the performance of its students.

I was angry with his acceptance of the certificate because the principal deserves none of the credit for the improvement in math scores. My colleagues and I developed the new approach that heightened student enthusiasm for studying math and led directly to the improved test scores. When we presented the plan to the principal two years ago, he did not think it would work and refused to allocate funds for the new math counselor that we sought. We went ahead in spite of his opposition and all put in extra hours ourselves to perform the tasks of the math counselor we were never able to hire. Our new approach worked. For the principal to accept credit for something he opposed and to do so without even mentioning our initiative and extra effort is simply wrong. No one should ever take credit for something that he opposed. I think I should schedule a meeting with the chair of the board to lay out the facts and get them to see what kind of an unethical person the principal really is.

Do you agree with this approach?

2. I was put in an awkward situation recently when my principal overheard me talking to a colleague about the teachers association's issues committee meeting last week. When I ran into her in the bathroom later that day, she said she had heard that there had been an association issues meeting and wanted to know what it was about. She and I have had a pretty good relationship, but many of the teachers find her arrogant and dictatorial; and her leadership style was the primary topic at the meeting. But I didn't want to tell her that, so I said that I had only been able to stay at the meeting for few minutes because I had a doctor's appointment and had to leave early. That wasn't true, but at least it saved me from having to violate the confidentiality of the meeting and from getting into what I'm sure would have been an uncomfortable conversation with my principal.

Was it okay that I responded as I did?

3. One day, I was pretty sure that an eighth grader in my middle school science class was on drugs. He was behaving erratically and had a kind of spacey look. My

suspicion was confirmed when I heard a student in the class whisper to another that the boy in question had bragged to her that he was using.

Following the policy of the school, I went to the principal and expressed my assessment that this boy was on drugs. The principal indicated that I had done the right thing by telling her and said she would call the parents immediately, which she did. When the parents heard the accusation about their son, they were livid—but at me, not at their son. They said, "There is absolutely no reason for her to make that accusation. She has no evidence. It is obvious this teacher is out to get our son."

The next day the boy did not come to my class, but I saw him exiting from another science class in the room across the hall. I asked the other teacher what was up, and he said the boy had been transferred into his class that morning. I could only conclude from this that the principal did not want to get into a dispute with the boy's parents and saw the transfer as an easier way to deal with the matter than to stand up for me or my assessment of his drug use. I felt abandoned and angry. Now I wonder what, if anything, I should do about this.

4. I was coming to the end of my first year as social studies department chair at the high school. It was a challenging year, but on the whole, I felt as if I had made progress in building mutually respectful relations with most of the teachers and in getting us thinking about improvements in our curriculum. The last thing I needed was the news about Bob.

Bob had been a history teacher at the school for nearly three decades. This was his last year and a big retirement party was planned for him after graduation in June. He has always been very popular with students and his colleagues hold him in very high regard. He is diligent about his teaching responsibilities and a pleasant colleague. So it came as a surprise to me when a girl in his senior American history class came to me and reported that Bob had been sending her almost daily e-mails in which he described his growing affection for her. At first, she said, she had been excited that her favorite teacher was giving her this much attention. But then the e-mails became increasingly explicit and she began to feel uncomfortable. Now she can hardly look at him in class without thinking about those e-mails. She wants to be transferred out of his class or she wants me to tell him to stop the e-mails. I asked her if she had copies of his e-mails, but she said she had been so upset by them two nights earlier that she had trashed them all. I also asked her if she had spoken with her parents about this, and she said, "I'd never do that; they think he's a great teacher and they would just blame me."

There are just two weeks left in the school year. I am afraid if I make a big issue out of this that I will offend a lot of the teachers because they are good friends with Bob. It would be a shame to have an honorable 30-year career besmirched by an indiscretion at the very end—if the student's charges are, in fact, true. It would be awkward to transfer the student without explaining to Bob why I was doing that. It would also force me to explain to the other teacher into whose class she was transferred why I was doing that so late in the semester.

What should I do?

5. I have been the chorus director at our high school for more than a decade. I share an office off the practice room with Silvio, the band director. We have worked together

for most of the time I've been at the school. We're not friends, and he can be tempestuous from time to time. Nevertheless, we've developed a reasonably good professional relationship.

Last week, the principal asked me to come to her office for a chat. When I did, she told me that she had good reason to suspect that Silvio had been misappropriating funds that the band boosters had raised for new instruments. I asked what she meant by "misappropriating." She looked at me very seriously and said, "I think he's been stealing some of the money and keeping it for himself."

I asked how she knew this, and she replied that she had information from a very reliable source that she couldn't identify. But all she had was this accusation, no evidence. Knowing Silvio's temper, she did not want to confront him about this until she had proof that he was guilty of wrongdoing. "This is where you can help," she said. "I'd like you to look through Silvio's desk drawers when he's not there. He keeps the records there of his instrument purchases and the money he gets from the band boosters. I'd like to see if the amount of money he's spending on instruments equals the amount that's been raised. I don't have a right to ask him for this since it's not part of my budget; it's all private donations. All I need you to do is to find the totals and write down what you find. You don't need to take any of the records, just look at them.

"I hate to ask you to do this," she went on, "but it would raise suspicions if anyone else was in your office. But if you'll help me with this, I'll be sure to stand up for you when the school board goes through its annual exercise of cutting our budget next spring. You know how vulnerable the chorus program was last year."

How should I respond?

10

The Teacher, Superintendent and School Board, and the Community

When immigrants poured into America from eastern and southern Europe at the end of the 19th century, schools were the place where they first confronted and adapted to the language and mores of their new country. When the civil rights movement unfolded in the United States in the middle decades of the 20th century, schools were a primary battleground. When women began to demand equal treatment and fair play, schools were often the place where their demands first arose and were first met. And now in the 21st century, with technology bringing radical changes in our lives, what used to be regarded as radical lifestyles gaining acceptance, and the very definition of childhood in flux, once again schools are the place where community traditions most often confront the forces of change (Goodlad, 2004; Graham, 2005; Jackson, Davis, Abeel, & Bordonaro, 2000).

No school is an island. Schools are communities within communities. They have their own habits and procedures, their own goals and constraints. But they also reflect and sometimes have to deflect the values and demands of the residential communities they inhabit. In a diverse and changing country, schools often become the landscape where new values confront the old, new realities have to be superimposed on traditional understandings (Marshall & Oliva, 2006). The tension between schools and the communities that support them is natural and inevitable (Goodlad, 2004; Graham, 2005). And it is a constant source of ethical challenges for teachers and school leaders.

In this chapter, we look at some of the ways that schools and communities interact and some examples of the complications inherent in those relationships. In these cases, we will see that sometimes the values and expectations of the broader community are imposed on schools in ways that counter the values or objectives of the school. We will see, too, that teachers who live in a community sometimes find that its citizens do not respect the separation between their professional and private lives. And we will observe that those who hold positions of political power in a community may sometimes regard their authority as an opportunity to pressure school leaders to act in ways that are contrary to their professional obligations. Good relations between schools and their communities are mutually beneficial, but—as these cases suggest—they are rarely easy and almost never uncomplicated.

THE GIRLS IN THE HALL

Marsville is a small conservative community. Many of the citizens attend the large Assembly of God church. There are many boundary issues in a town like this because everyone knows what everyone else is doing. What happens in school rarely stays in school.

So things became complicated the month before school ended when a ninth-grade girl and an eleventh-grade girl were caught kissing in various places in the high school. They were seen in the conference room, bathrooms, and hallways. When the principal confronted them, they told her they were dating.

Both sets of parents are embarrassed by this relationship and now have restraining orders against each other and the girls. Both sets of parents are angry with the school and are threatening to sue if the administration does not put an end to this relationship. Since the principal shares their concern, she raised it as Topic A at a recent faculty meeting. She asked all of the teachers to monitor the movements of the older student and to make sure the two students are separated at all times.

This was troubling to Margaret, an experienced teacher who just moved to Marsville with her family the previous summer. Margaret respects the deeply held values of the community even though she does not share all of them. But she did not think that would be a problem at school. Now, it seems she was wrong.

Margaret believes that the principal has overreacted to this relationship between students because they are of the same gender. She has already noticed that many students at the high school are in relationships with students of the opposite sex and the public displays of affection in the school are not uncommon. There does not seem to be any official reaction to those. So, it seems clear to Margaret that the concern about the two girls is precisely because they are both girls. That seems wrong and discriminatory. In Margaret's view, all students should be treated equally. If visible expressions of affection between the two girls are to be proscribed, so should similar expressions between students of the opposite sex.

Margaret decides to raise her concern with Jonathan, her department chair. A native of Marsville, he has been teaching at the school for more than a decade, so Margaret thinks he will be a good source of advice. Jonathan listens to Margaret's concerns, and then a smile comes over his face. "Now you're getting to know the real Marsville," he says. "Even those of us who've always lived here think this is a pretty narrow-minded community. But it has its charms, and those outweigh some of the values we don't all share. You'll just never win on this one, Margaret; it's going to be a long time before gay lifestyles are tolerated here. We might wish it were otherwise, but there's nothing we can do about it. The school has to reflect the values of the community, and those values are pretty powerful here. If you challenge them, you'll just be jeopardizing your own career and maybe making this a pretty uncomfortable place for you and your family to live."

What should Margaret do now?

Discussion

There are two issues here that offer Margaret different approaches to addressing her concerns. The first of those is the school's treatment of the girls involved in a same-sex relationship. Here the school administration seems to reflect the predominant values in the community: Such relationships are wrong and the school should take steps to prevent them. If Margaret thinks this is discriminatory, her first recourse might be to determine whether the school's handling of this matter violates any public policies. Antidiscrimination policies vary widely among states and localities; in some places, it is unlawful to discriminate on the basis of sexual orientation. If that is the case in Marsville or the state where Marsville is located, then Margaret could surely bring that to the attention of school administrators.

If no such policy exists, and the school is not acting unlawfully, than Margaret's primary recourse here is educational: to attempt to alter the values of the school and perhaps of the community by enlightening her colleagues and other community members about the need to respect diverse lifestyles. That may be an uphill struggle, but changing community values is never easy.

A potentially more effective approach for Margaret is to raise questions about the school's policy on public displays of affection. If it is wrong for two students of the same gender to display their affection for each other in school, so should it be wrong for students of the opposite sex to do so. That is the core of fairness and equal treatment. Margaret could suggest to the faculty council or to the administration that an explicit policy be developed that treats all public displays of affection similarly, regardless of who is involved. This would not alleviate all of the negative attention the two girls at the center of this case receive, but at least it would afford them the knowledge that the school is not treating them unfairly or unequally in constraining their expressions of affection for each other.

THE FUND RAISER

Staceyville likes to refer to itself as "a town that takes pride in itself." One of the reasons for that is that years ago when the state would not provide funding for a new elementary school, citizens of Staceyville worked hard to raise the money themselves and to build their own school. They used every kind of fund raising opportunity they could find, and contractors in the town provided much of the labor without charge. Over the entrance to the school is a sign that says, "The school we built together for our children."

Now, as the entire country faces a financial crisis, Staceyville is forced again to rely on its own resources. The tax base in town is shrinking and the state has been cutting back on its annual subsidies to local schools. At a recent meeting of the school board, the members were much moved by a description that an older community member provided of the effort that went into building the elementary school. At the end of this presentation, the board chair asked, "Why can't that same spirit save us now as we face this financial challenge?"

After further discussion, the board decided to sponsor a series of fundraisers to collect money that would go directly into the annual school budget. One of the board members who moved to town not long ago recommended a school carnival in which teachers would wear funny costumes and submit to various forms of good-humored humiliation for which townspeople would pay. There would be a dunk tank, for instance, where a teacher would sit above a tank of water and anyone who paid a couple of dollars to pull a lever could dump the teacher into the water.

And there would be a pie-in-the-face contest where paying contestants could put whipped cream pie in the face of a teacher whose head was stuck through a hole in a sheet. There would also be three-legged races, a pig wrangle, teacher karaoke, and a variety of other events.

To most of the teachers, the carnival sounded like fun. If it would raise money to cover the budget shortfall, that was even better. But two of the younger teachers did not share this view. To them, participating in such an event was undignified and embarrassing and had nothing to do with the educational tasks for which they were hired. So they went to the president of the teachers' union and expressed their reservations.

She listened carefully and sympathetically to their concerns, and then responded, "I hear you on this. But I have to ask that you go along with the rest of us. These are trying times for all of us, and it's in our best interests to look like we're willing to go the extra mile to help the community through the financial crisis. After all, we're the ones who will ultimately benefit because the money that the carnival raises will go right into the school budget."

One of the teachers replied, "We understand that, but we think you need to draw a line somewhere. How much humiliation does a teacher have to endure in order not to be an outcast? We don't want to cause trouble, but we believe we have a right to our dignity and our professional status, and having pies thrown in our faces violates that right. There are many things we'd be happy to do—a charity softball game, for instance, or a barbecue or an auction—those don't cross the line into humiliation. But we don't want to cross that line."

A few days later, the union head ran into the chair of the school board at the grocery store. He told her how excited he was about the carnival and how appreciative he was of the teachers' willingness to participate in it. But when the union head described to him the objections of some of the teachers and their suggestions for other ways to raise money, he replied, "None of those other things would bring in much dough," said the school board chair. "People in this town don't care about auctions or softball games. But they would turn out in droves for the carnival. You tell those teachers that we expect everybody to be a good sport about this, and those who aren't—well, we'll know who they are if the budget shortfall requires us to RIF (reduction in force) anybody."

The union head wonders what she should do now. What advice would you give her?

Discussion

The ethical issue at the center of this case is whether the school board can properly expect school employees to perform services for which they have not contracted. And if they are reluctant to perform those services, may it punish them? The board chair's threat about

RIFs clearly suggests a willingness to punish those teachers who do not participate in the carnival. Is this ethical trespassing?

Teachers and other school employees often do things that go beyond contractual requirements (Bryk & Schneider, 2002). Sometimes these are educational, sometimes extracurricular, sometimes even in the form of community service. There is nothing wrong with that so long as the noncontractual services are voluntary. But that is not the case here. While one can understand the desire of teachers to help the community through a financial crisis, especially in light of their self-interest in preventing major cuts in the school budget, they may not all agree about how best to provide that help.

This does not appear to be a case in which the teachers, individually or collectively, volunteered to organize a carnival. Others made that decision, and they assumed the teachers would go along. And while many teachers seem willing to do that, they have no right to force their unwilling colleagues to do so. The two who are reluctant to be "humiliated" have offered to contribute their services in other ways, but are not willing to cross a line between dignity and humiliation. Their opinion deserves respect.

Perhaps the best course for the union head is to call a meeting to discuss this issue and the concerns of the two teachers. She should be especially concerned, as should her colleagues, about the threat suggested by the chair of the school board. A communication to the board in which the union indicates its willingness to help in raising private funds to cover the shortfall in the school budget but demands participation in the decisions about how those funds will be raised seems an appropriate response here. And even if it is decided to go ahead with the carnival, it appears that the union should protect the two concerned teachers by finding roles for them that do not put their dignity at risk.

Contracts have meaning. They define the boundaries of the relationship between school boards and school employees. When employees are asked or expected to perform noncontractual services, especially when there is a community expectation that they will, they are entitled to participate in discussions about the nature of those services and to freely express their willingness or reluctance to perform them. School boards ought not to be mere echoes of community expectations; they have an obligation as well to protect school employees when those expectations become unreasonable or unduly burdensome (Bryk & Schneider, 2002).

THE MAGIC OF LEARNING

Jessica is a second-grade teacher in Springvale. She is also a single mother with two children aged 8 and 10. After her husband died in a car accident three years ago, she has struggled to make ends meet. Her situation improved, though, when a friend introduced her to the Magic of Learning.

The Magic of Learning is a "teaching program," a mix of videos, software, and a magazine subscription designed to improve the learning skills and ultimately the test scores of elementary school-age students. Jessica began as a trainee, following some of the experienced salespeople as they went door to door seeking to convince families to purchase the Magic of Learning program. When she was ready, she began to make the sales pitches on her own. This fall, she purchased the franchise for all of Springvale. She recruits others, especially teachers, to work for her, but Jessica still makes sales calls two nights a week when her sister can take care of the children.

Early in her association with the company, Jessica learned that the easiest targets for sales of the Magic of Learning are the parents of children in her own classes. Many of them found it hard to resist when their child's teacher came to the door offering a program that would improve their classroom performance. Whether they actually believed the program was useful or not, some of them no doubt thought their teacher would be more inclined to help their children if they purchased this item she was selling. When she was recruiting others to work for her, Jessica found that teachers were her best candidates because they too would have the same advantage.

One day, Mr. Morris, Jessica's principal, and Ms. Jameson, the district's superintendent, asked her to meet with them after school. They told her that Mr. Morris had received a complaint from the parents of one of the children in her class about Jessica showing up at their door in the evening trying to sell them some "junk educational products." They told the principal that this felt like extortion. They felt that if they did not buy what Jessica was selling she would be in a position to take it out on their child. The father of the child said, "It was almost as if she were trying to get bribes to treat the children of those who bought the Magic of Learning more favorably than those who did not."

Jessica had imagined that she would be questioned about this one day, and she had a prepared response. "I don't think I'm doing anything wrong," she told them. "First, I believe in this program. I think it does genuinely and legitimately help children to learn. I wouldn't sell something I didn't believe in. Second, I think I'm well within my rights to do something like this on my own time. I have two children I'm solely responsible for, and it's hard to make ends meet. Of all the ways I could make outside income, this seems to fit most comfortably and appropriately with the rest of my life. What I'm doing by selling the Magic of Learning is really, ultimately, no different from what I do every day at school.

(Continued)

(Continued)

"And in terms of selling to the parents of children I teach, there's no pressure. Just like any other potential customers, they can look over the product and decide whether they want to buy it or not. There is no shred of evidence that my work with anybody's children is affected by whether they buy this product or not. I have the franchise for Springvale, I only sell in Springvale, and among those who live in Springvale are parents of some of the children I teach. They are by no means my only potential customers. So I don't think I have anything to apologize for, nor do I think you have any right to prevent me from earning outside income in this way which is perfectly legal, perfectly open, and no threat to the values of the school.

"Besides," Jessica continued, "lots of teachers earn money beyond their teaching income. One of my colleagues paints houses in the summertime. I know for a fact that he has painted the houses of several people who have students in the school. A high school teacher—you know who he is—sells cars on the weekends. I'm sure he must've sold cars to people who have children in the school. Now those are men. I'm thinking maybe we have a different policy here for men than for women. It's okay for men to make money outside of school, even if their customers are parents of children in the school, but it's not okay for women? I'm having trouble seeing what exactly it is that I'm doing wrong that's different from what the men have been doing for a long time."

After listening to Jessica's response, Mr. Morris and Ms. Jameson said they would need to think about it further and they would talk later. What should they do now?

Discussion

There are two issues the school administrators need to sort out here. One is the matter of the kinds of activities in which teachers in schools may appropriately participate on their own time. The other is the matter that Jessica raised about gender discrimination in the implementation of such a determination.

Few school administrators are likely to want to be in the position of having to make day-to-day determinations about which outside activities are appropriate for teachers in their schools. A much better approach is to develop a policy through negotiations with teachers, their union, and appropriate school officials. Then when questions of this sort arise, an administrator can refer to the policy as the basis for a determination (Enomoto & Kramer, 2007; Pellicer, 2003).

But let us assume that in this case no such policy has been developed, and Mr. Morris and Ms. Jameson have to decide whether

Jessica's employment is appropriate. We can also assume that teachers are permitted to earn income outside of school as long as they do so on their own time and without compromising their school responsibilities. The question then becomes: Is there something about the way Jessica is earning outside income that poses a problem and, if so, what must be done to resolve that problem?

Jessica maintains that selling a learning program to clients in Springvale, including parents of children she teaches, is no different from selling automobiles or painting houses where the occasional client will also be the parent of a student. But that claim is hard to sustain here. First, those who sell automobiles or paint houses rarely go door to door to solicit business. If a teacher who painted houses in the summer, for example, went door to door and especially to the doors of parents whose students he taught, that might well raise a different concern than if he simply placed an advertisement in the local newspaper that he was available to paint houses. And an automobile salesman who spends his time on the car lot waiting for customers to drive in surely is not putting any special pressure on parents of students he teaches. There may be parents who choose to buy a car from that salesperson because they think he may then treat their child more favorably in school, but that is a long line of dots to connect and, therefore, difficult to define as a potential conflict of interest for the teacher.

Jessica's case seems categorically different. She is not painting houses or selling automobiles. She is selling a program which she tells parents will be valuable to them as a supplement to their children's learning. But as the teacher whose evaluation of the children's performance will be the most important measure of how they are learning, she has an apparent conflict of interest (Strike, 2007). It would be hard for her not to be tempted to give more attention to the children whose parents bought her program and to raise their grades as proof that the program she is marketing does, in fact, work.

And there's another problem, potential abuse of her position. She may not be trying to extort purchases of her program from the parents of the children she teaches, but it is not surprising that some of them perceive her actions in that way. They feel undue pressure to buy the program, not because they believe in its value, but because they think that buying it will improve the teacher's assessment of their children's work or that not buying it will diminish that assessment. In other words, they would feel compelled to respond differently to a sales pitch from Jessica—because she is the teacher of their children—than they would to a salesperson they did not know. One could reasonably conclude that Jessica is taking improper advantage of her position as a teacher for her own personal financial gain.

In the absence of a school policy to guide them, the school administrators would be well served by consulting with other administrators in other school districts to seek their advice on how to respond in this case. A sensible response, it seems, would recognize that there is a wide variety of income-earning activities perfectly appropriate for teachers on their own time, yet the integrity of the school needs to be protected. And critical to that protection is a prohibition on teachers engaging in any income-earning activity that does or might appear to take advantage of their positions as teachers, especially as a teacher of the children whose parents they are directly soliciting as clients.

That Jessica is approaching the parents of her students by showing up at their doorsteps and that she is trying to sell them a program that focuses on the education of their children clearly seems to violate these proscriptions. The problem is not that she is earning income on her own time or even that she is earning income by marketing a learning program. The problem is that she is marketing it directly to the parents of her students who often feel unduly pressured. The school administrators should tell Jessica that she may continue to sell the Magic of Learning, but she cannot approach the parents of her current students or any she is likely to teach in the future or in any other way seem to suggest to them that they should purchase the Magic of Learning from her.

The issue of gender discrimination seems much clearer and easier to resolve. The policy of the school with regard to outside income-earning opportunities for teachers should apply equally to all teachers regardless of gender. If Jessica has legitimate evidence that men and women are being treated differently in matters of the sort, she should do as she has done here and indicate that to the administrators. If she continues to feel that such discrimination exists and they have not responded satisfactorily, then she should raise her concerns with the school board or her union representative.

A MARKED MAN

It was the worst day of his life when the two cops showed up in the music room. That room had been Patrick's second home for more than a decade. As the music director at Montrose Middle School, Patrick had spent hundreds of rewarding hours teaching instrumental music to young students and somehow organizing them into bands whose performances thrilled their parents. Now to have these two detectives telling him that he was being charged with a crime made the whole facility seem somehow alien, even hostile.

One of the girls in his classes, a 13-year-old named Meredith, had told her parents that Patrick had touched her inappropriately when he was showing her how to hold a saxophone. And she said he did not just do it once, he did it every day for a week until she told him to stop. The detectives told Patrick this was a violation of state law; they told him the name and number of the statute under which he was being charged; and then they read him his rights before they began to question him. He denied ever touching Meredith or any other student inappropriately and said he had a long track record of proper dealings with students that would certainly show that he was not guilty of this charge.

Nevertheless, the detectives put him in the police car, took him to the station, and booked him on the charge of sexual abuse of a minor. Though it would be terribly expensive, Patrick chose to hire his own attorney rather than take a public defender, and he began to fight the charges.

He found, however, that few people sided with him, even old friends. Some people in his family, it seemed, also began to keep their distance. The school superintendent put him on administrative leave. He would be paid during the period until the charges were resolved, but he was not permitted to be on the school grounds nor to have any contact with any of the students in his music classes.

The investigation continued for several weeks, with extensive interviewing of other students and of Patrick's colleagues. It was the most humiliating thing he had ever endured, and there was almost nothing he could to do about it. He and his attorney found it very difficult to prepare his defense. How do you prove you have not done something, when a 13-year-old girl says you have, and there are no other witnesses?

The trial was scheduled to begin on April 14. On April 13, Patrick received a call from his attorney who said that Meredith had just recanted her story and refused to testify in the trial. Therefore, the county attorney had no choice but to drop all the charges. Patrick was free.

When Patrick went back to work, his principal said to him, "I owe you an apology, Patrick, but I know that will never be enough to make up for the difficult things you've experienced. I should've been on your side from the beginning, and I should have stood up for you. I really regret that I didn't do that. It's not just that I believe in innocent until proven guilty, I know that Meredith is a flighty young girl who's had a history of lying. Plus, I've worked with you for a long time, and I should have known that you never would have done anything like what you were charged with. You may never be able to forgive me for the way I mishandled this; I just hope we can work together and get beyond this."

Patrick thanked the principal for his words and said, "No hard feelings. I know what a difficult position this put you in. Like you, I just want to put it behind me and move forward."

But the matter was far from settled. At the school board meeting later that week, a number of parents showed up to protest Patrick's return to teaching.

(Continued)

(Continued)

Many of them felt that even though Meredith said that she made up the charges against him and refused to testify, she was probably scared of being on the witness stand. They contended that there had to be some substance to the charges. They did not want their children subjected to Patrick as music teacher. They demanded that the school board not reinstate him.

The board chairman said that the board could not prevent the reinstatement. Patrick had not been convicted of any crime, and, therefore, under the law and the union contract he could not be deprived of his teaching position. One of the other board members, sympathetic to the parents, noted that in the last round of budget cuts the future of the music program was very much on the table. It had survived that round, but the board member suggested that if Patrick were reinstated one solution would be to cut the entire middle school instrumental music program in the next round. Two of the other members of this five-member board then followed with statements of concurrence.

As the superintendent listened to all this, it seemed clear to him that if Patrick were reinstated then three of the five members of the school board would vote to eliminate the music program at the earliest opportunity. Instrumental music is popular with the parents whose children are in it, and their effective organizing is what saved it in the last round of budget cuts. Now the superintendent is perplexed. What should the superintendent do?

Discussion

In most school settings, Patrick's entitlement to his teaching position would be established in the union contract negotiated through collective bargaining. The superintendent would have no authority to fire him without cause. Since he was not convicted of a crime, it is unlikely that adequate cause exists here for his removal. Beyond that, there is the cherished value of innocent until proven guilty. There is no proof of Patrick's guilt in this case, and he is entitled to be treated as if he is innocent, which, in fact, he may well be.

School superintendents often find themselves pressured by school boards, or some members of school boards, to take actions that they believe to be wrong. In this case it appears that some members of the school board are threatening to make a decision not on the substantive merits of an issue but rather as a way to force the superintendent's hand in a personnel matter.

The proper response for the superintendent in this case is to state the facts clearly before the board. He should note that under the contract that the teachers union negotiated with the board he has no authority to remove Patrick from his position because he has not been found guilty of any crime or wrongdoing. He might also note that for the board to accomplish that outcome by eliminating the entire instrumental music program, in his view, would be a violation of the spirit of the contract with long-term harmful consequences for relations between the teachers' union and the board.

Then he might note that the future of the instrumental music program has been under discussion for some time and, no doubt, will continue to be. But as the appointed leader of the school system he will make recommendations to the board about the future of that program based on budget considerations and the substantive value of the program relative to other budget choices and not as a substitute for any personnel action that he or the board or anyone in the community might desire.

There is the risk, of course, that this kind of clear statement might present political problems for the superintendent. The three members of the board seeking Patrick's dismissal might lose confidence in the superintendent and his own position might soon be at risk. But that is a consideration that superintendents often have to recognize. They make decisions and recommendations with which school boards or some of their members disagree; sometimes they make decisions that may appear to defy the wishes of some members of the school board. But if they make those decisions openly and with the best interests of the school system at heart, and if they explain them clearly to all their constituents, then they will have been doing the job for which they were hired (Fullan, 2003). There may be political costs for that, but their ethical responsibilities will be richly fulfilled.

The cases in this chapter have dealt primarily with ethical dilemmas for school boards and superintendents. They are meant to be instructive for teachers as well. Just because they are not closely connected to a situation and are not the ones making the decisions does not mean teachers can afford to be neutral.

As teachers, as educators, we have a duty to think about ethics and act ethically all the time. Our ethical responsibilities may cause discomfort or worse to others, but our greatest responsibility is to do the best we can for all children by making schools and the actions of people in them sensitive to the ethical issues in policies and their implementation.

For Reflection and Conversation

The following are cases similar to the ones presented in this chapter. How would you analyze the individual's obligations and what might be appropriate next steps for teachers or administrators to take?

❖ ❖ ❖

1. Jane Stokely, the high school principal, had been very clear with the student speakers at graduation this year that they could not include any mention of or reference to religion in their speeches because of Supreme Court decisions banning prayers at public graduations. She defined appropriate public discourse boundaries, so that no one would cross them, even unintentionally. She even refused to let one student speak when he declined to promise that his speech would be nonreligious.

But then at graduation came the time for traditional remarks from the chair of the school board, a clergyman in this community where religion is strong. At the end of his talk, he asked the audience to bow their heads in silence and thank the Lord "for the gift of these wonderful young people." At the end of the silence, he said, "We pray that you keep them safe in the years ahead and that they all live fulfilling lives in Christ. In Jesus' name we pray. Amen." After the ceremony, several students whose speeches were censored protested to Jane. They had the support of several teachers, including one who was Jewish, who thought the prayer not only wrong but deeply offensive.

What should Jane do? What should the teachers who were offended do if they are unhappy with Jane's response?

2. Lydia has not had an easy go of it. She has been in foster care most of her life, moving from household to household. At age 16, she moved in with her boyfriend, Jon, and lived at his parents' house. Despite their reservations about two 16-year-olds cohabiting, they thought Lydia was a good influence on Jon, who had been a rather aimless child.

Remarkably, in spite of her erratic personal life, Lydia had always taken school seriously. It was the one place where she thought people, teachers especially, really cared about her, and she wanted to please them by working hard. She also just enjoyed reading and solving problems and other aspects of learning. Several of her teachers thought she would be a candidate for admission to a good college and that she should be able to get a full scholarship. One of them, Allison Ames, her math teacher, had almost become her personal advocate and guiding star.

So it was a great disappointment to Allison when Lydia came to see her after school one day to tell her that she was pregnant. Lydia said her plan was to stay in school through her pregnancy, but then she would need to find a job because Jon's parents did not want a baby in the house even though Jon was the father and it would be their grandchild. His parents had told her they thought both of them were too young to be parents and that Lydia should get an abortion. "You don't agree with them, Ms. Ames, do you?" Lydia asked.

How should Allison respond?

3. The school board worked hard to spread the pain when the budget crunch forced it to reduce the school budget last year by three percent. But this year, an even larger cut will be necessary, and there is no way to reach its bottom line without terminating several extracurricular programs. The board decided the fairest way to do this was to calculate the per-pupil cost of maintaining athletic, theater, music, and other extracurriculars, then to cut those that served the fewest students at above-average costs.

One of those on the list to be cut was the swimming program. The school had no pool of its own, and the cost of renting time for practices and meets at the local college pool was too much to justify its continuance. In early December, the board announced the cuts it would make for the following year. One of them was the swimming program.

A few days later, Martin Harris, a lawyer in town, called the superintendent and offered to fund the entire swimming program out of his own pocket for the next five years (even after his own daughter, a senior and the current swimming captain, has graduated). He said he would invest the total funds needed for five years in an account at the local bank and give access to that account to the athletic director as long as the superintendent would pledge that the funds be used only for the intended purpose—to fund swimming.

Should the superintendent accept this gift? What does he say to other parents if they object that sports for their children were cut and they can't afford to pay for their restoration? Is it fair for the school to accept funds for one sport while canceling others?

4. To earn some extra income to be sure he can meet his monthly child support payments, Charlie works on Saturday nights as a bouncer at a local bar. Charlie is a third-grade teacher in the town where the bar is located. This bar has an especially sleazy reputation. The place has also been summonsed on several occasions for serving under-age patrons, including two girls from the high school. It even lost its liquor license for a month once for repeated violations of the drinking age.

The principal believes it is inappropriate for a teacher to work in a place with this kind of reputation, especially as the bouncer, which means he is often standing visibly outside. He speaks to Charlie and asks him to quit this job. Charlie protests and says it's his free time and he can do what he wants. The principal responds that no teacher has a totally free hand in taking on outside work, not when the reputation of the school is jeopardized and not when the work seems to undermine lessons the school is trying to teach.

You are a friend of Charlie's and a teacher in the school. Charlie comes to you and asks you to speak to the principal in his defense. What do you do?

5. John had long believed that students learn not merely from the formal instruction they receive in their classes but also from the messages that schools provide in the way they operate. So he was deeply distressed at a decision the school board handed down at its meeting last week.

His community had been losing population in recent years and the shrinking tax base combined with a declining number of pupils had caused the school board to make some cuts in the number of teachers. One of the places where cutting seemed desirable was in the business program at the high school. Fewer students are interested in business classes, and the board concluded that laying off a teacher would not weaken the offerings in that department. Following the normal practice of RIFing, the most recently hired teacher was more complicated here because there were two teachers, hired on the same day and with virtually identical performance evaluations, who had the least seniority in the department. There was, however, a significant difference between them. One was Caucasian and one was African-American.

Because the school board had long been committed to affirmative action in its personnel policies, it decided to lay off the teacher who was Caucasian. In the eyes of the board, this was no different from choosing between two teaching candidates of equal qualifications in the hiring process. Affirmative action practices would dictate in such a case that the job should be offered to the African-American candidate.

This situation posed a profound dilemma for John. He supported the community's affirmative action policy, but the business teacher who was to be laid off as a result of the board's decision was John's close friend. She came to him in distress when the decision was announced and sought his advice. One potential recourse here was for her to file a lawsuit against the school board claiming that she was a victim of reverse discrimination and that she had been denied the "equal protection of the laws" guaranteed to all citizens under the 14th amendment. She asks for John's advice on whether she should proceed with such a lawsuit. What advice should John give?

6. Together, Mountainside Middle and High schools serve nearly a dozen communities spread over a vast geographical area in a rural county. For as long as anyone could recall, the policy at these two schools had been to allow teachers to request their course schedules by seniority. That meant that those who had taught the longest had significant influence over their schedules while the newest teachers had little or none. Because many teachers had long commutes to school and because there were many months in the middle of the year when the weather was often difficult, the senior teachers nearly always preferred to start their day with a preparation period so that they did not have to arrive at school as early as those who had first-period classes. This made commuting easier for them.

Several of the younger teachers were talking about this in the faculty lounge and decided that the policy was unfair. Senior teachers already made more money than the junior teachers and to afford them the additional benefit of more control over their schedules seemed to magnify the gap between older and younger teachers at Mountainside. They decided to approach the superintendent and raise this issue, asking that he change the policy so that seniority would no longer affect scheduling. What they proposed instead was that teachers' names be drawn from a hat and that those whose names were drawn first would be given priority in decisions about scheduling for the following year.

If you were the superintendent in this case, what implications would you consider in deciding, whom would you consult and how, and what would you decide?

11

Summing Up

Our interest in this subject is rooted in a belief we hold firmly: Schools cannot succeed in their primary missions without consciously developing a sturdy ethical culture. Indeed, developing and maintaining such a culture is one of the primary missions of any school. Our commitment to write this book grew out of an equally strong belief: Fulfilling that mission is not easy.

For education professionals, meeting ethical responsibilities is always a work in progress, not something one studies for a time and then masters. Each day brings new issues and new challenges. Some fit familiar profiles, some create new ones. Acting ethically requires constant attention.

In this book, we have tried to offer guidance to teachers and administrators in recognizing the ethical challenges they confront and in developing reasonable responses to them. We began by identifying some bedrock ethical principles as useful touchstones in finding the "right" course of action when faced with complex and appealing alternatives.

- *The Golden Rule.* Do unto others as you would have them do unto you. Treat everyone with respect, even those with whom you disagree.
- *The Rule of Benevolence.* Act in ways that produce the greatest good or the least harm for the greatest number. Judge your acts by their outcomes, especially when confronting choices that all have some potentially negative consequences.

- *The Rule of Universality.* Remember that no act is so inconsequential that acting unethically is irrelevant. Judge your actions by their propriety, not their magnitude. Before acting, ask yourself: Would it be acceptable if everyone acted this way?
- *The Rule of Publicity.* An unethical action remains unethical even if no one sees it. If uncertain about the propriety of a course of action, pose these questions: Would it be acceptable if everyone knew about it? Could you justify the action to your children or your boss?

We have also noted throughout this book how easy and sometimes comforting it can be to deny that an ethical choice exists or to rationalize evasion of ethical responsibilities. Most of us regard ourselves as responsible adults who always act ethically. That creates the false confidence that any choice we make is ethically correct simply because we are ethical and we have made the choice. But self-interest, convenience, and habit too easily blind us to the character of our actions or prevent us even from considering the possibility that we may be wrong.

Often the greatest challenge to the ethical culture of any school is the people with primary responsibility for developing and maintaining it: us. We cross ethical boundaries not because we consciously choose or intend to do that. But when we fail to recognize the ethical implications of our actions or too readily rationalize them away, we undermine the high standards that we and our schools profess. Recall the excuses we use to evade ethical obligations. "Everyone does it." "No one will notice." "It's only a little thing." "It's not illegal." "No harm, no foul." "It helps people even if it's wrong." "No problem. I'm an honest person." "They owe me this. I work so hard, and they pay me so little."

The cases in this book cover a wide range of behavior (and misbehavior). They are not easily summed up, at least not without missing much of the nuance that is part of every complex ethical quandary. But there are some recurring themes that might serve as red flags for any teacher or administrator. Whenever confronted with one of these situations, it is prudent to step back, think about the broader implications of the choices we face, and consult with others before proceeding:

- Using public property or resources for private purposes
- Deceiving students or colleagues, even for what may seem to be a valid purpose
- Violating the law

- Breaching school policies
- Profiting personally from school-based relationships with students or their families
- Telling tales out of school about students or colleagues
- Violating confidences

There may be occasions when an action can be appropriate even if it seems to bypass one of these red flags, but in such cases especially, one should proceed with great caution and only after consulting with appropriate and reliable people before acting.

Ultimately, the ethical culture of any school is the sum of the sensitivities and behaviors of all of its inhabitants. Doing the right thing is something all of us must think about constantly, not simply as an abstract standard but as a guide to all of the choices we face as educators. If we take this responsibility seriously, if we seek constantly to discern the ethical implications of our actions, if we share our doubts with and request the advice of our colleagues, and if we reflect broadly on our errors, our schools will be healthier workplaces. And our students will learn one of the best lessons we can teach them: that constant pursuit of our ethical obligations is never simple but always necessary.

Resource A

Workshop Outline: Tools for Teachers and Teacher Leaders

We provide this agenda for a day of delving into ethical issues and helping participants analyze situations and develop some understanding of how best to deal with them. We provide times to indicate the amount of time to allot to each item; however, one could easily spend more time on each item and thus have the program last an entire eight-hour day if that is desirable.

9:00 a.m.   Introductory Remarks (Purposes and Goals of the Workshop)

9:15 a.m.   Facilitated Discussion of Ethical Principles and Decision Rules

- What is an ethical issue? How do you know you're confronting one?

- Ethical challenges in schools
  o Knowing and obeying the law
  o Conflict of interest
  o Misuse or abuse of position
  o Nonschool employment or business
  o Memberships and affiliations
  o Civility

- Principles of ethical behavior
  o Golden rule
  o Rule of benevolence

  o Rule of universality
  o Rule of publicity

10:30 a.m. Break

10:45 a.m. Discussion of Cases

- Use cases at the end of each chapter of this book
- Almost all of the cases can be analyzed using the principles enumerated in the book; in fact, it is useful to try to apply all of the ethical lenses so that participants develop a sense of what the principles are and how they play out in differing situations
- We suggest using ones that seem most appropriate to the participants and their experience

11:45 a.m. Participants Develop Their Own Cases

Ask participants to provide a written description of one or more situations where they have had to confront a significant ethical issue. These should be sufficiently anonymous that they can be discussed by the workshop later in the day. Alternately, the program conveners might ask participants to develop a critical event as described in the protocol in Resource B.

Noon Lunch Break

(During the lunch break the facilitator can review the situation descriptions provided by participants and organize them for use in the afternoon discussion.)

1:00 p.m. Discussion of Situations Provided by Workshop Participants

Depending on the size of the group, this kind of discussion can be in small groups or with the entire group of participants. It is useful to make copies of the cases so that each group is discussing the same case.

2:15 p.m. Open Discussion of Issues Raised During the Day

2:30 p.m. Facilitator's Closing Remarks and Guidance

Alternately, the group can generate ideas that can augment the book in providing guidance. This kind of list makes the principles more concrete and relevant to the participants.

Resource B

Examining Critical Events

Examining a critical event in your own professional life is a way to discover your core beliefs. It can also provide insights into useful ways to resolve conflicts you may experience with regard to fundamental philosophical differences—within yourself or between you and other teachers. Developed by the National School Reform Faculty, the Critical Incident Protocol provides a process for developing and assessing an ethical case from one's own experience through a structured conversation with colleagues.

We have adapted the protocol so that it involves writing about an experience that is problematic because one is unsure how to proceed, especially since it prompts the participant to wonder about the ethical dimensions of a situation. An individual shares the situation, being careful to present the facts and to stop before he or she starts analyzing or reflecting on the situation.

Listeners to the presentation ask clarifying and probing questions; then, as in many protocols, the presenter is silent while he or she listens to others discuss the ideas presented and tease out the ethical issues they see. Finally, the entire group participates in a discussion of the problem, not trying to solve it but rather to explore fully the possible approaches to thinking through the ramifications of various responses and actions.

This kind of protocol can be used as the jumping off point for individual platforms of beliefs or for ongoing sharing and learning with regard to skill and cognitive development around ethical thinking. Teachers could use the protocol with a group where they each share a critical event in a session or where individuals have the floor for an entire session and each person's event is fully examined.

The protocol, and many others, can be downloaded from **http://www .nsrfharmony.org/protocol/learning_adult_work.html**. As with most protocols, we suggest that they be used in the context of ongoing learning communities so that teachers feel safe in exposing their thoughts and beliefs and, at the same time, trust the legitimacy of questions and critique of their peers.

The University of Maine Educational Leadership Faculty has developed a process for reflective writing that, in a similar vein to the Critical Incident Protocol, helps students analyze incidents in their own lives. Students use the form to clarify events for themselves, then share their understanding with others who will add their insights and provide feedback.

We suggest that people use the form below to look at an incident where the writer has concerns about the ethical implications of a situation. The writer may also wonder about the social and political implications, too, so the reflection may help to surface and explore those as the writer seeks ways to resolve an interpersonal or intrapersonal conflict.

Adapted Critical Event Reflective Journal Entry

Focus: Think about an encounter today or in the last few days that in retrospect raised some ethical questions or challenges for you. Note the time and place of the critical event.

Describe: Recall the details of the experience: What was said, what you felt. Try to re-create and thus relive the experience. Write down all of the details you can remember. Now, give the bird's eye view (from the balcony) and the insider's view.

Time:	Place:	Participants:
Bird's Eye View: **What was said and done**		**Insider's View:** **What I thought and felt**

Reflect: Reflect on what the experience means to you now. What do you understand more clearly about the ethical, social, or political implications, as well as your beliefs and values? Write down these understandings for yourself.

_____

_____

_____

_____

_____

Reconstruct: Consider the implications these insights have for your practice as you continue to wrestle with the ethical issues surfaced in this event. In what ways do you anticipate acting, thinking, and feeling differently?

_____

_____

_____

_____

_____

Draw up a specific action plan for your immediate next steps for dealing with this specific issue and the people and events involved in it.

_____

_____

_____

_____

_____

References

Ackerman, R. A., & Mackenzie, S. V. (2007). *Uncovering teacher leadership: Essays and voices from the field.* Thousand Oaks, CA: Corwin.

American Library Association/American Association of School Libraries. (2001). *Program standards school library media specialist preparation.* Retrieved January 8, 2009, from www.ncate.org

Ayers, W. (2004). *Teaching toward freedom: Moral commitment and ethical action in the classroom.* Boston: Beacon Press.

Bandura, A. (1986). *Social foundations of thought and action; a social cognitive theory.* Englewood Cliffs, NJ: Prentice Hall.

Bandura, A. (1999). *Self-efficacy in changing societies.* Cambridge, UK: Cambridge University Press.

Barth, R. S. (2001). *Learning by heart.* San Francisco: Jossey-Bass.

Barth, R. S. (2006, March). Improving relationships within the schoolhouse. *Educational Leadership, 63*(6), 8–13.

Berlak A., & Berlak, H. (1981). *Dilemmas of schooling: Teaching and social change.* New York: Methuen.

Blase, J., & Anderson, G. L. (1995). *The micropolitics of educational leadership: From control to empowerment.* New York: Teachers College Press.

Blase, J., & Blase, J. (2002, December). The dark side of leadership: Teacher perspectives of principal mistreatment. *Educational Administration Quarterly, 38*(5), 671–727.

Bryk, A., & Schneider, B. (2002). *Trust in schools: A core resource for school improvement.* New York: Russell Sage Foundation.

Chaleff, I. (2003). *The courageous follower: Standing up to and for our leaders* (2nd ed.). San Francisco: Berrett-Koehler.

Committee on Intellectual Property Rights and the Emerging Information Infrastructure. (2000). *The digital dilemma: Intellectual property in the information age.* Computer Science and Telecommunications Board Commission on Physical Sciences, Mathematics, and Applications, National Research Council. Retrieved January 8, 2009, from http://www.nap.edu/openbook.php?record_id=9601

Dewey, J. (1915). *The school and society.* Chicago: University Press.

Donaldson, G. A. (2006). *Cultivating leadership in schools: Connecting people, purpose, and practice* (2nd ed.). New York: Teachers College Press.

Donaldson, G. A., & Sanderson, D. (1996). *Working together in schools: A guide for educators.* Thousand Oaks, CA: Corwin.

DuFour, R., Eaker, R., & DuFour, R. (Eds.). (2005). *On common ground: The power of professional learning communities.* Bloomington, IN: National Education Service.

Enomoto, E. K., & Kramer, B. H. (2007). *Leading through the quagmire: Ethical foundations, critical methods, and practical applications for school leadership.* Lanham, MD: Rowman & Littlefield Education.

Evans, R. (1996). *The human side of school change; reform, resistance and the real-life problems of innovation.* San Francisco: Jossey-Bass.

Freire, P. (2004). *Pedagogy of the oppressed.* New York: Continuum.

Fried, R. L. (2001). *The passionate teacher: A practical guide.* Boston: Beacon Press.

Fullan, M. (2003). *The moral imperative of school leadership.* Thousand Oaks, CA: Corwin.

Fullan, M. (2004). *Leadership and sustainability: System thinkers in action.* Thousand Oaks, CA: Corwin.

Fullan, M., & Hargreaves, A. (1996). *What's worth fighting for in your school?* New York: Teachers College Press.

Goddard, R. D., Hoy, W. K., & Woolfolk-Hoy, A. (2000). Collective teacher efficacy: Its meaning, measure, and impact on student achievement. *American Educational Research Journal, 37*(2), 479–507.

Goleman, D., Boyatzis, R., & McKee, A. (2002). *Primal leadership: Realizing the power of emotional intelligence.* Boston: Harvard Business School Press.

Goodlad, J. I. (2004). *A place called school: Prospects for the future.* New York: McGraw-Hill.

Graham, P. A. (2005) *Schooling America: How the public schools meet the nation's changing needs.* New York: Oxford University Press.

Jackson, P. W., Boostrom, R. E., & Hansen, D. T. (1998). *The moral life of schools.* San Francisco: Jossey-Bass.

Jackson, A., Davis, G. A., Abeel, M., & Bordonaro, A. (2000). *Turning points 2000: Educating adolescents in the 21st century.* New York: Teachers College Press.

Johnson, D. R., & Johnson, F. P. (2005). *Joining together: Group theory and group skills* (9th ed.). Boston: Allyn and Bacon.

Keith-Spiegel, P. M., Whitley Jr., B. E., Balogh, D. W., Perkins, D. W., & Wittig, A. F. (2002). *The ethics of teaching: A casebook* (2nd ed.). Mahwah, NJ: Lawrence Erlbaum.

Kidder, R. A. (2003). *How good people make tough choices: Resolving the dilemmas of ethical living.* New York: Harper Paperbacks.

Lortie, D. (1975). *Schoolteacher: A sociological study.* Chicago: University Press.

Marshall, C., & Oliva, M. (2006). *Leadership for social justice: Making revolutions in education.* New York: Pearson Education.

Meier, D. (1995). *The power of their ideas: Lessons for America from a small school in Harlem.* Boston: Beacon Press.

Meier, D. (2002). *In schools we trust: Creating communities of learning in an era of testing and standardization.* Boston: Beacon Press.

Nash, R. J. (1996). *"Real world" ethics: Frameworks for educators and human service professionals.* New York: Teachers College Press.

Palmer, P. (2007). *The courage to teach: Exploring the inner landscape of a teacher's life*. New York: John Wiley & Sons. (Original work published 1997)

Pellicer, L. O. (2003). *Caring enough to lead: How reflective thought leads to moral leadership* (2nd ed.). Thousand Oaks, CA: Corwin.

Plante, T. G. (2004). *Do the right thing: Living ethically in an unethical world.* Oakland, CA: New Harbinger Publications.

Sergiovanni, T. J. (1992). *Moral leadership: Getting to the heart of school improvement*. San Francisco: Jossey-Bass.

Shapiro, J. P., & Gross, S. J. (2008). *Ethical educational leadership in turbulent times: Re(Solving) moral dilemmas*. New York: Lawrence Erlbaum.

Shapiro, J. P., & Stepkovich, J. A. (2005). *Ethical leadership and decision making in education: Applying theoretical perspectives to complex dilemmas*. New York: Lawrence Erlbaum.

Simpson, C. (2005). *Copyright catechism: Practical answers to everyday school dilemmas*. Worthington, OH: Linworth.

Sizer, T., & Sizer, N. (1999). *The students are watching: Schools and the moral contract*. Boston: Beacon Press.

Sockett, H. (1990). Accountability, trust, and ethical codes of practice. In J. I. Goodlad, R. Soder, and K. A. Sirotnik (eds.), *The moral dimensions of teaching*, pp. 224–250. San Francisco: Jossey-Bass.

Starratt, R. (2005). *Ethical leadership*. San Francisco: Jossey-Bass.

Strike, K. A. (1990). The legal and moral responsibility of teachers. In J. I. Goodlad, R. Soder, and K. A. Sirotnik (eds.), *The moral dimensions of teaching*, pp. 188–223. San Francisco: Jossey-Bass.

Strike, K. A. (2007). *Ethical leadership in schools: Creating community in an environment of accountability*. Thousand Oaks, CA: Corwin.

Strike, K. A., & Soltis, J. F. (1998). *The ethics of teaching* (3rd ed.). New York: Teachers College Press.

Tschannen-Moran, M. (2004). *Trust matters: Leadership for successful schools.* San Francisco: Jossey-Bass.

Wei, R. C., Darling-Hammond, L., Andree, A., Richardson, N., & Orphanos, S. (2009). *Professional learning in the learning profession: A status report on teacher development in the United States and abroad.* Dallas, TX: NSDC.

Index

CORWIN

A SAGE Company

The Corwin logo—a raven striding across an open book—represents the union of courage and learning. Corwin is committed to improving education for all learners by publishing books and other professional development resources for those serving the field of PreK–12 education. By providing practical, hands-on materials, Corwin continues to carry out the promise of its motto: **"Helping Educators Do Their Work Better."**